Samuel Green

The Boundary Lines of Old Groton

Samuel Green

The Boundary Lines of Old Groton

ISBN/EAN: 9783337312909

Printed in Europe, USA, Canada, Australia, Japan

Cover: Foto ©ninafisch / pixelio.de

More available books at **www.hansebooks.com**

The Boundary Lines

OF

Old Groton.

BY

SAMUEL A. GREEN, M.D.

Remove not the ancient landmark, which thy fathers have set.
Prov. xxii. 28.

GROTON, MASS.
1885.

University Press:
JOHN WILSON AND SON, CAMBRIDGE.

To the Memory

OF

JONATHAN DANFORTH,

WHO SURVEYED THE ORIGINAL GROTON PLANTATION;

And to the Memory of the Chainmen,

WHO, THOUGH UNKNOWN TO US EVEN BY NAME, ACCOMPANIED HIM THROUGH
THE WILDERNESS DURING HIS WEARISOME LABORS,

THIS BOOK IS INSCRIBED

By the Author.

CONTENTS.

		PAGE
I.	GROTON PLANTATION	9
II.	NASHOBAH AND LITTLETON	19
III.	GROTON GORE AND THE PROVINCIAL LINE	32
IV.	WESTFORD AND HARVARD	45
V.	DUNSTABLE, HOLLIS, AND NOTTINGHAM	53
VI.	PEPPERELL	72
VII.	SHIRLEY, TYNGSBOROUGH, AND AYER	82

INDEX 99

ILLUSTRATIONS.

GROTON AND NEIGHBORHOOD, 1885 . . . . *Frontispiece*
GROTON PLANTATION 13
GROTON GORE 33

THE BOUNDARY LINES OF OLD GROTON.

I.

GROTON PLANTATION.

WELL-DEFINED boundaries are of the highest importance to communities as well as to individuals. In the one case they mark the limits of political power, and in the other of landed possession. Oftentimes such boundaries prevent strifes and quarrels, and thus indirectly and silently promote the Christian virtues. During the various stages of civilization, from the earliest days of recorded history, they have been considered absolutely essential to the existence of society; and in the Mosaic code of laws a curse was uttered against the man who should remove his neighbor's landmark. The ancient Romans personified this principle of fixed boundaries, and deified him under the name of Terminus. A temple was built in his honor, where he was worshipped by the pagans.

The various transfers of territory connected with the town of Groton, in its corporate capacity, have a certain local interest, and in order to gratify it this little book is printed.

The original grant of the township was made by the General Court on May 25, 1655, and gave to the proprietors a tract of land eight miles square; though during the next year this was modified so that its shape varied somewhat from the first plan. It comprised all of what is now Groton and Ayer, nearly all of Pepperell and Shirley, more than one half of Dunstable, a large part of Littleton, smaller parts of Harvard and Westford, Massachusetts, and a portion of Nashua, New Hampshire, besides a little patch of Hollis, in the same State. The grant was taken out of the very wilderness, relatively far from any other town, and standing like a sentinel on the frontiers. Lancaster, fourteen miles away, was its nearest neighbor in the southwesterly direction on the one side; and Andover and Haverhill, twenty and twenty-five miles distant, more or less, in the northeasterly direction on the other. No settlement on the north stood between it and the settlements in Canada. Chelmsford and Billerica were each incorporated about the same time, though a few days later. For several years previously, however, there had been some scattered families living at Billerica, then known as Shawshin.

When the grant was made, it was expressly stipulated that Mr. Jonathan Danforth, of Cambridge, with such others as he might desire, should lay it out with all convenient speed, in order to encourage the prompt settlement of a minister; and furthermore that the selectmen of the town should pay a fair amount for his services. During the next year a petition, signed by Deane Winthrop and seven others, was presented to the General Court, asking for certain changes in the conditions, and among them the privilege to employ another "artist" in the place of Mr. Danforth, as he was overrun with business. The petition was referred to a committee, who reported favorably upon it, and the request was duly granted. Formerly a surveyor was called an artist, and in old records the word is often found with that meaning.

Ensign Peter Noyes, of Sudbury, was then engaged by the grantees, and he began the survey; but his death, on September 23, 1657, delayed the speedy accomplishment of the work. It is known that there was some trouble in the early settlement of the place, growing out of the question of lands, but its exact character is not recorded ; perhaps it was owing to the delay which now occurred. Ensign Noyes was a noted surveyor, but not so famous as Jonathan Danforth, whose name is often mentioned in the General Court records, in connection with the laying out of lands and towns, and many of whose plans are still preserved among the Archives in the State House. Danforth was the man wanted at first for the undertaking ; and after Noyes's death he took charge of it, and his elder brother, Thomas, was associated with him. The plat or plan of the land, however, does not appear to have been completed until April, 1668. The survey was made during the preceding year. At a meeting of the selectmen of the town, held on November 23, 1667, it is recorded that a rate should be levied in order to pay " the Artest and the men that attended him and his diet for himself and his horse, and for two sheets of parchment, for him to make two platts for the towne, and for Transportation of his pay all which amounts to about twenty pounds and to pay severall other town debts that appear to us to be due."

It was of Danforth that the poet sang : —

> He rode the circuit, chain'd great towns and farms
> To good behavior ; and, by well-marked stations,
> He fixed their bounds for many generations.
> His art ne'er fail'd him, though the loadstone fail'd,
> When oft by mines and streams it was assail'd.
> All this is charming, but there's something higher,
> Gave him the lustre which we most admire.

This poetical tribute to his character is taken from a poem written at the time of his death, and appears in Farmer and Moore's " Collections " (ii. 65). The allusion in the last line is to his piety.

A little further on in the records a charge of five shillings is made "ffor two sheats of Parchment." These entries seem to show that two plans were made, — perhaps one for the town and the other for the Colony ; but neither copy is now to be found. An allusion is made to one of them in a petition, presented to the General Court on February 10, 1717, by John

Shepley and John Ames. It is there stated that "the said Plat thô something defaced is with the Petitioner;" and furthermore "That in the year 1713 Mr Samuel Danforth Surveyor & Son of the aforesaid Jonathan Danforth, at the desire of the said Town of Groton did run the Lines & make an Implatment of the said Township laid out as before & found it agreeable to the former. W^h last Plat the Petitioners do herewith exhibit, And pray that this Honble Court would allow & confirm the same as the Township of Groton."

Plans were needed by the public authorities, to show officially what lands had already been appropriated. Sometimes one grant would overlap or conflict with another, and thus create confusion. The grant of five hundred acres lying within the limits of Groton Plantation, and made to Major Simon Willard in the spring of 1657, was given under a misapprehension. The General Court had no official knowledge that this tract had previously been taken up, as at that time no plan of the original plantation had been returned to that body, or even made. Years afterward the mistake was recognized by the authorities, and an equivalent of land allowed to the proprietors for their loss. At a very early period in the history of the Colony, there was an order regulating the laying out of grants, so that places fit for townships should not be spoiled for that purpose, but the order was frequently violated.

All the early surveys of public grants were very liberal, and purposely included more territory than was given by the General Court. Land was cheap, and did not belong to private individuals. Sometimes an excess was taken to make up "for rocks and waste land," and this was permitted by the authorities. Danforth's survey was no exception, and gave the proprietors ample measurements. Over and above this fact, the difficulty of defining lines of boundary with precision is never wholly overcome, unless it is done by landmarks successively visible from one another. Surveys dependent on the compass are always subject to many sources of inaccuracy, such as the loss of magnetic virtue in the poles of the needle; blunting of the centre-pin; unsuspected local attractions; oversight or

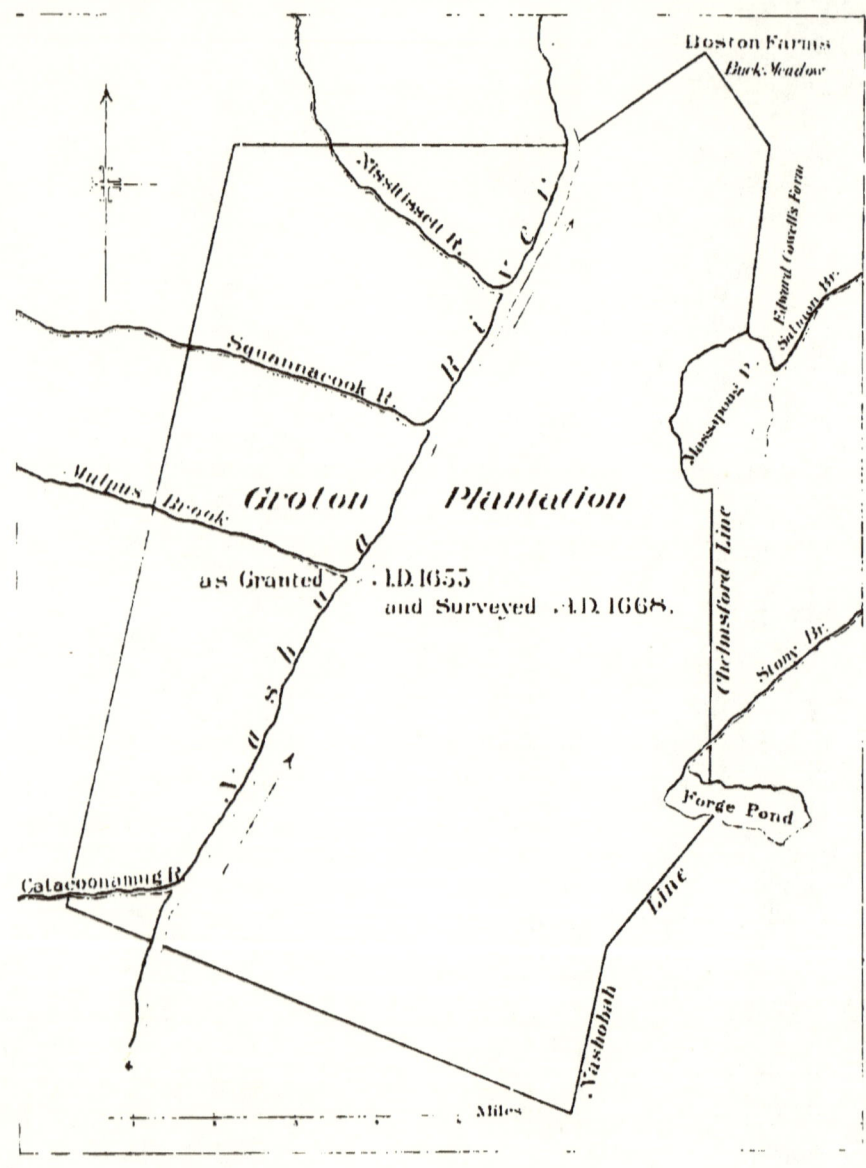

mistake as to the secular variation, and variability from the influence of the sun, known as the diurnal variation, to say nothing of the elements of uncertainty connected with the chain. Error from the diurnal variation may amount, in the distance of a mile, to twenty feet or more of lateral deviation. Under these circumstances it is neither fair nor just to subject the work of the early surveyors to the test of modern methods.

While the original plan of Groton has been lost or destroyed, it is fortunate that many years ago a copy was made, which is still preserved. In June, 1826, the Honorable James Prescott was in the possession of the original, which Caleb Butler, Esq., at that time transcribed into one of the town recordbooks. Even with this clew a special search has been made for the missing document, but without success. If it is ever found it will be by chance, where it is the least looked for. There is no reason to doubt the accuracy of the outlines or the faithfulness of the copy. The relative distances between the streams emptying into the Nashua River, however, are not very exact; and in the illustration placed opposite, for the sake of clearness I have added their names, as well as the name of Forge Pond, formerly called Stony Brook Pond.

Accompanying the copy is a description of the survey, which, in connection with the drawing, gives a good idea of the general shape of the township. Probably in the original these two writings were on the same sheet. In the transcript Mr. Butler has modernized the language and made the punctuation conform to present usage. In the illustration I have followed strictly the outlines of the plan, as well as the course of the rivers, but I have omitted some details, such as the distances and directions which are given along the margins. These facts appear in the description, and perhaps were taken from it by the copyist. I have also omitted the acreage of the grant, which is grossly inaccurate.

Whereas the Plantation of Groton, containing by grant the proportion of eight miles Square, was begun to be laid out by Ensign Noyes, and he dying before he had finished his work, it is now finished, whose limits and bounds are as followeth,

It began on the east side of Nashua River a little below Nissitisset hills at the short turning of the River bounded by a pine tree marked with G. and so running two miles in a direct line to buckmeadow which p{{r}}tains to Boston Farms, and so is bounded by Boston Farms, Billerica land and Edward Cowell's farm until you come to Massapoag Pond, which is full of small islands; from thence it is bounded by the aforesaid Pond until you come to Chelmsford line, after that it is bounded by Chelmsford and Nashoboh lines until you come to the most southerly corner of this Plantation, and from thence it runs West-North-West five miles and a half and sixty four poles, which again reacheth to Nashua River, then the former west-north-west line is continued one mile on the west side of the river, and then it runs one third of a point easterly of north & by east nine miles and one quarter, from thence it runneth four miles due east, which closeth the work to the river again to the first pine below Nissitisset hills, where we began: it is bounded by the Farms and plantations as aforesaid and by the wilderness elsewhere; all which lines are run and very sufficiently bounded by marked trees & pillars of stones: the figure or manner of the lying of it is more fully demonstrated by this plot taken of the same.

By JONATHAN DANFORTH,

April 1668. Surveyor.

The Nissitissett Hills are conspicuous elevations in the northeast quarter of the town of Pepperell, standing on the west side of the Nashua River, perhaps half a mile distant from it; and just below them the river takes a decided bend to the westward. The largest of these hills is situated near the village of East Pepperell, and to this day is known in the neighborhood as the Nissitissett; while north of it are two other hills, which extend to the present State line, and form prominent landmarks when seen from the east side of the river.

These bearings give very nearly the position of "a pine tree marked with G," from which Danforth started in making his survey. It was undoubtedly very near to the present State line, and probably just north of it. From the pine-tree the boundary ran northeasterly two miles in a straight line to Buck Meadow, which is a well-known locality, still bearing the same name. From this boundary the description gives neither distance nor direction to the next angle, but the plan shows it very well. Apparently the course was about a mile and a half in the southeasterly direction. It is difficult now to understand why the original grant was laid out along its northern border in so irregular a manner, but perhaps it was owing to the character of the soil or the topography of the country.

A carefully constructed map of the region, based on these facts, includes within its limits the present Lovewell's Pond, which is an excellent guide in tracing this boundary running in a southeasterly direction. The pond lies so near the line that I thought it might be possible still to identify it in part by some modern mark, such as a fence, road, or stone wall; and I determined to reconnoitre the district. On reaching the neighborhood one hot afternoon in August, 1884, I found, much to my gratification, a road, little more than a cart-path, and substantially straight, running along a natural ridge for half a mile, coinciding with this line. The ridge is a marked feature of the region, and would naturally have been taken by Danforth as a boundary. The road is a very old one, and known in the vicinity as the Ridge Road. While near one end of it, I met a young man, of whom I inquired the name of the meadow, just in front of us, when he at once replied: "It hain't got no name, but the folks 'round here call it Buck Meadow." This bit of information was confirmed by several persons living in the neighborhood. The whole of the triangle made by Danforth's two courses, with the present State line as a base, comes now within the territory of Nashua, New Hampshire.

The lands known as "Boston Farms, Billerica land, and Edward Cowell's farm," were all granted by the General Court after the incorporation of Groton, but before the date of the survey, which will account for their appearance in the description.

It was undoubtedly Danforth's intention to make the eastern boundary of Groton correspond in part with the western boundary of Chelmsford, though the territory of the last-named town never extended to Massapoag Pond. At the time of the survey there was a tract of unappropriated land between the pond and the northern boundary of Chelmsford, which afterward was included within the township of Dunstable, but now is in Tyngsborough. Danforth's line was continued through Forge Pond, and then made to follow the boundary of Nashobah, an Indian grant, which subsequently was included in Littleton. It passed on, nearly a mile further, in a straight course, until the southeast corner of Groton Plantation was reached. This corner is now represented by an angle in the boundary between Boxborough and Harvard, perhaps two hundreds rods south of the Littleton line. Here a prominent ridge, belonging to the Oak Hill range, comes to an end; and Danforth, in his survey, was not slow to use as a landmark such a conspicuous feature in the topography of the country. From this place the line turned and ran "West-North-West five miles and a half and sixty-four poles," where it crossed the Nashua River, and then continued another mile, on the west side of the river, to the southwest corner of the plantation. This point is known to-day as "Groton Old Corner," and the stone post marking the boundary is lettered on the top : —

GROTON &
STOW LEG
OLD CORNER

The post stands in the woods very near the Leominster road, about a mile from Shirley Village. From here the line ran in a northeasterly direction for nine miles, to a place where the northwest corner of the township was reached. The stone post marking the spot comes now very near the boundary of Addison Wood's farm in Pepperell, and is still called "Groton Old Corner." From this point the line ran due east for four miles to the pine-tree on the banks of the Nashua River, whence Danforth started to make the survey. It undoubtedly crossed the river a short distance north of the present State line, and passed through the southeast corner of the present town of Hollis.

The description of the original grant of Dunstable has been twice printed, but with so many inaccuracies and interpolations that I am constrained to print it again for the third time. The original copy, in the handwriting of Jonathan Danforth, surveyor, is found on the first page of the earliest book of Dunstable town records, now in the possession of the city of Nashua. The leaf on which it is written is much torn and worn near the front edge. Of the first line about three quarters of an inch is gone, and near the middle of the edge probably an inch and a quarter is also gone. Without attempting to supply the missing letters or words, I have placed brackets thus [ ] to indicate them, which in some lines are very evident. The following copy was made by me with much care on June 5, 1885, and it is here given line for line with the original:—

THE NEW PLANTATION GRANTE
APON MERIMACK REUER

It Lieth on both sids merimack Riuer on the n[   ]
Riuer it is bounded by Chelmsford on the south by [   ]
partly by Cuntry land the Line runing from the boun[   ]
du north Ten mile untill you Come to Souhegon Riuer [   ]
Called dram Cup hill to a great Pine ny to ye said Riuer: a[   ]
of Charlstown Scoole farm bounded by Souhegon Riuer
North and on the east Sid merrimacke : It begins at a great che[   ]
             corner of
which was supposed to be near the northern Mr Brintons land
and from thence it Runs sou south east six ^miles to a Pine [   ]
with : F : standinge within sight of Beauer Broke
It Runs two degres west from the ~~the~~ south four mile and ouer [   ]
which Reached to the ~~to=the~~ ~~to=the~~ south side of henery [   ]
ffarme at Jeremies Hill then from y^e South-East angell of [   ]
it runs two degres and a quartor westward of the south [   ]
of the long Pond which lieth at y^e head of Edward Co[   ]
And thus it is Bounded by the said Pond and the head of th[   ]
Takeinge in Captaine Scarlets farme to that bou[   ]
All which is sofficiantly Bounded and described [   ]
danforth Suruayer: 3^m: 1674:

The map of Old Dunstable, between pages 12 and 13 in Fox's History of that town, is very incorrect, so far as it relates to the boundaries of Groton. The Squannacook River is put down as the Nissitissett, and this mistake may have tended to confuse the author's ideas. The southern boundary of Dunstable was by no means a straight line, but was made to conform in part to the northern boundary of Groton, which was somewhat angular. Groton was incorporated on May 25, 1655, and Dunstable on October 15, 1673, and no part of it came within the limits of this town. The eastern boundary of Groton originally ran northerly through Massapoag Pond, and continued into the present limits of Nashua, New Hampshire.

II.

NASHOBAH AND LITTLETON.

On the southeast of Groton, and adjoining it, was a small township granted, in the spring of 1654, by the General Court to the Nashobah Indians, who had been converted to Christianity under the instruction of the Apostle Eliot and others. They were few in numbers, comprising perhaps ten families, or about fifty persons. During Philip's War this settlement was entirely deserted by the Indians, thus affording a good opportunity, which was not lost, for the English to encroach on the reservation. These intruders lived in the neighboring towns, but mostly in Groton. Some of them took possession with no show of right, while others went through the formality of buying the land from the Indians; though such sales did not, as was supposed at the time, bring the territory under the jurisdiction of the towns where the purchasers severally lived. It is evident from the records that these encroachments gave rise to controversy. The following entry, under date of June 20, 1682, is found in the Middlesex Court Records (iv. 38) at East Cambridge, and shows that a committee was appointed at that time to re-establish the boundary lines of Nashobah : —

Capt. Thomas Hinchman, L[t]. Joseph Wheeler, & L[t]. Jno. flynt surveyo[r], or any two of them are nominated & impowred a Comittee to rune the ancient bounds of Nashoboh Plantaccon, & remark the lines, as it was returned to the geñall Court by said m[r] flynt at the charge of the Indians, giveing notice to the select men of Grotton of time & place of meeting, wch is referred to m^r flint, to appoynt, & to make return to next Couñ Court at Camƀr in order to a finall settlem^t.

Again, under date of October 3, 1682 ("3. 8. 1682."), it is entered that —

The return of the comittee referring to the bounds of Nashobey next to Grotton, was p'sented to this Court and is on file.
Approued

The "return" is as follows: —

We Whose names are under written being appointed by ye Honord County Court June: 20th 1682. To ruñ the Ancient bounds of Nashobey, haue accordingly ruñ the said bounds, and find that the town of Groton by theire Second laying out of theire bounds have taken into theire bounds as we Judge neer halfe Indian Plantation Severall of the Select men and other inhabitants of Groton being then with us Did See theire Erro^r therein, & Do decline that laying out So far as they haue Invaded the right of ye Indians.

Also we find y^t the Norwest Corner of Nashobey is ruñ into ye first bounds of Groton to ye Quantity of 350 acres according as Groton men did then Show us theire Said line, which they Say was made before Nashobey was laid out, and which bounds they Do Challenge as theire Right. The Indians also haue Declared them Selves willing to forego that Prouided they may haue it made up upon theire West Line. And we Judge it may be there added to theire Conveniance.

JOSEPH WHEELER
JOHN FLINT

2 : Octob^r : 1682.
Exhibited in Court 3 : 8 : 82 :
& approued T D : R.

A true Coppy of ye originall on file wth ye Records of County Court for Middx.

Ex^d p^r Sam^{ll} : Phipps Cle

[Massachusetts Archives, cxii. 331.]

Among the Groton men who had bought land of the Nashobah Indians were Peleg Lawrence and Robert Robbins.

Their names appear, with a diagram of the land, on a plan of Nashobah made in the year 1686, and found among the Massachusetts Archives, in the first volume (page 125) of "Ancient Plans Grants &c." Lawrence and Robbins undoubtedly supposed that the purchase of this land brought it within the jurisdiction of Groton. Lawrence died in the year 1692; and some years later the town made an effort to obtain from his heirs their title to this tract, as well as from Robbins his title. It is recorded that the town, at a meeting held on June 8, 1702, —

did uote that they would giue Peleg larraness Eairs three acers of madow whare thay ust to Improue and tenn acers of upland neare that madow upon the Conditions following that the aboue sd Peleg larrances heirs do deliuer up that Indian titelle which thay now haue to the town

At the same meeting the town voted that —

thay would giue to robart robins Sener three acers of madow where he uste to Improue: and ten acers of upland near his madow upon the Conditions forlowing that he aboue sd Robart Robbins doth deliuer: up that Indian titels which he now hath: to the town.

It appears from the records that no other business was done at this meeting, except the consideration of matters growing out of the Nashobah land. It was voted to have an artist lay out the meadow at "Nashobah line," as it was called, as well as the land which the town had granted to Walter and Daniel Powers, probably in the same neighborhood; and also that Captain Jonas Prescott be authorized to engage an artist at an expense not exceeding six shillings a day.

Settlers from the adjacent towns were now making gradual encroachments on the abandoned territory, and among them Groton was well represented. All the documents of this period relating to the subject show an increased interest in these lands, which were too valuable to remain idle for a long time. The following petition, undoubtedly, makes a correct representation of the case: —

To his Excellency Joseph Dudley Esq! Captain Gen!! & Governour in Chief in & over her Majesties Province of the Massachusets Bay &c : togeither with the honourable Council, & Representatives in Great and Gen!! Court Assembled at Cambridge Octobe! 14th 1702.

The Petition of the Inhabitants of Stow humbly sheweth.

That Whereas the honourable Court did pleas formerly to grant vnto vs the Inhabitants of Stow a certain Tract of Land to make a Village or Township of, environed wth Concord, Sudbury, Marlbury, Lancaster, Groton, & Nashoby : And Whereas the said Nashoby being a Tract of Land of four miles square, the which for a long time hath been and still is desert'd and left by the Indians none being now resident there, and those of them who lay claim to it being desireous to sell said Land ; and some English challenging it to be theirs by virtue of Purchase ; and besides the Town of Groton in particular, hath of late extended their Town lyne into it, takeing away a considerable part of it ; and Especially of Meadow (as wee are Well informed) Wherefore wee above all o! Neighbour Towns, stand in the greatest need of Enlargement; having but a pent up smale Tract of Land and very little Meadow.

Whence we humbly Pray the great & Gen!! Court, that if said Nashoby may be sold by the Indians wee may have allowance to buy, or if it be allready, or may be sold to any other Person or Persons, that in the whole of it, it be layed as an Addition to vs the smale Town of Stow, it lying for no other Town but vs for nighness & adjacency, together with the great need wee stand of it, & the no want of either or any of the above named Towns. · Shall it Pleas the great & Gen!! Court to grant this o! Petition, wee shall be much more able to defray Publick Charges, both Civil, & Ecclesiasticall, to settle o! Minister amongst vs in order to o! Injoyment of the Gospel in the fullness of it. Whence hopeing & believing that the Petition of the Poor, & needy will be granted. Which shall forever oblidge yo! Petition's to Pray &c :

THO : STEEVENS. Cler :

STOW. Octobe! 12th 1702.   In the Towns behalfe

[Massachusetts Archives, cxiii. 330.]

This petition was granted on October 21, 1702, on the part of the House of Representatives, but negatived in the Council, on October 24.

NASHOBAH AND LITTLETON. 23

During this period the territory of Nashobah was the subject of considerable dispute among the neighboring towns, and slowly disappearing by their encroachments. Under these circumstances an effort was made to incorporate a township from this tract and to establish its boundaries. The following petition makes a fair statement of the case, though the signatures to it are not autographs : —

To His Excel[y] Joseph Dudley Esq : Cap[t] Generall & Gov[r] in Chief in and over Her Maj[ties] Province of Mass[ts] Bay in New-England, Together with y[e] Hon[ble] the Council, & Representatives in Gen[ll] Court Assembled on the 30th of May, In the Tenth Year of Her Maj[ties] Reign Annoq Dom[i] 1711, — The Humble Petition of us the Subscribers Inhabitants of Concord, Chelmsford, Lancaster & Stow &c within the County of Midd[x] in the Province Afores[d].

Most Humbly Sheweth

That there is a Considerable Tract of Land Lying vacant and Unimproved Between the Towns of Chelmsford, Lancaster & Stow & Groton, as s[d] Groton was Survey'd & Lay'd out by Mr. Noyce, & the Plantation Call'd Concord Village, which is Commonly known by the Name of Nashoba, in the County of Midd[x] Afores[d]. & Sundry Persons having Made Entrys thereupon without Orderly Application to the Government, and as we are Inform'd, & have reason to believe, diverse others are designing so to do.

We Yo[r] Hum[ble] Petitioners being desirous to Prevent the Inconveniences that may arise from all Irregular Intrusions into any vacant Lands, and also In a Regular manner to Settle a Township on the Land afores[d]. by which the frontier on that Side will be more Clos'd & Strengthened & Lands that are at Present in no wise beneficiall or Profitable to the Publick might be rendred Servicable for the Contributing to the Publlick Charge, Most Humbly Address Ourselves to your Exc̄y : And this Honourable Court.

Praying that your Petitioners may have a Grant of Such Lands Scituate as Afores[d]. for the Ends & Purposes afores[d]. And that a Committee may be appointed by this Hon[ble] Court to View, Survey and Set out to Yo[r] Petitioners the s[d]. Lands, that so Yo[r] s[d]. Petitioners may be enabled to Settle thereupon with Such others as shall joyn them In an orderly and regular manner : Also Praying that Such Powers and Priviledges may be given and conferred upon the same as are granted to other Towns, And Yo^r Petitioners shall be Most ready to attend Such Directions, with respect to Such Part of the s^d. Tract as has been formerly reserv'd for the Indians, but for a Long time has been wholly Left, & is now altogether unimprov'd by them, And all other things which this Honble Court in their Wisdom & justice Shall See meet to appoint for the Regulation of such Plantation or Town.

And Yo^r Hum^ble Petitioners as in Duty Bound Shall Ever Pray &c.

Gershom Procter	Josiah Whitcomb
Sam^ll Procter	John Buttrick
John Procter	Willm Powers
Joseph Fletcher	Jonathan Hubburd
John Miles	Wm Keen
John Parlin	John Heald
Robert Robins	John Bateman
John Darby	John Heywood
John Barker	Thomas Wheeler
Saml Stratton	Sam^ll Hartwell, jun^r
Hezekiah Fletcher	Sam^ll Jones
	John Miriam

[Endorsed] In the House of Representatives
June 6: 1711. Read & Comitted.
7 ... Read, &
Ordered that Jon^a Tyng Esqr Thom^s Howe Esqr & Mr John Sternes be a Comittee to view the Lands mentioned in the Petition, & Represent the Lines, or Bounds of the severall adjacent Towns bounding on the s^d Lands and to have Speciall Regard to the Land granted to the Indians, & to make report of the quantity, & circumstances thereof.

Sent up for Concurrence.

JOHN BURRIL Speaker

In Council
June 7. 1711, Read and Concurr'd.

ISA: ADDINGTON, Sec^ry.

[Massachusetts Archives, cxiii. 602, 603.]

The committee to whom was referred this subject made a report during the next autumn; but no action in regard to it appears to have been taken by the General Court until two years later.

The report of the Comitty of the Honble Court vpon the petition of Concord Chelmsford Lancaster & Stow for a grant of part of Nashobe lands

Persuant to the directions giuen by this Honble Court bareng Date the 30th of May 1711 The Comity Reports as foloweth that is to say &ce

That on the second day of October 1711 the s^d comitty went vpon the premises with an Artis and veved [viewed] and servaied the Land mentined in the Peticion and find that the most southerly line of the plantation of Nashobe is bounded partly on Concord & partly on Stow and this line contains by Estimation vpon the servey a bought three miles & 50 polle The Westerly line Runs partly on Stow & partly on land claimed by Groton and containes four miles and 20 poll extending to a place called Brown hill, The North line Runs a long curtain lands claimed by Groton and contains three miles, the Easterle line Runs partly on Chelmsford, and partly on a farm cald Powersis farm in Concord; this line contains a bought fouer miles and seventy fiue poll

The lands a boue mentioned wer sheved to vs for Nashobe Plantation and ther were ancient marks in the severall lines fairly marked, And s^d comite find vpon the servey that Groton hath Run into Nashobe (as it was sheved to vs) so as to take out nere one half s^d plantation and the bigest part of the medows, it appeers to vs to Agree well with the report of Mr John Flint & Mr Joseph Wheler who were a Commetty imployed by the County Court in midlesexs to Run the bounds of said plantation (June ye 20th 82) The plat will demonstrate how the plantation lyeth & how Groton coms in vpon it: as allso the quaintete which is a bought 7840 acres

And said Comite are of the opinnion that ther may [be] a township in that place it lying so remote from most of the neighboreng Towns, provided this Court shall se reson to continew the bounds as we do judg thay have been made at the first laieng out And that ther be sum addition from Concord & Chelmsford which we are redy to think will be complyd with by s^d Towns

And s^d Comite do find a bought 15 famelys setled in s^d plantation of Nashobe (5) in Groton claim and ten in the remainder (and

3 famelys which are allredy setled on the powerses farm: were convenient to joyn w̃ s^d plantation and are a bought Eaight mille to any meting-house) Also ther are a bought Eaight famelys in Chelmsford which are allredy setled neer Nashobe line & six or seven miles from thir own meeting house

                                                                 JONATHAN TYNG
                                                                 THOMAS HOW
                                                                 JOHN STEARNS

In the House of Representatives
Nov^m 2: 1711. Read

Oct° 23, 1713.   In Council

Read and accepted; And the Indians native Proprietors of the s^d Planta^con Being removed by death Except two or Three families only remaining Its Declared and Directed That the said Lands of Nashoba be preserved for a Township.

And Whereas it appears That Groton Concord and Stow by several of their Inhabitants have Encroached and Setled upon the said Lands; This Court sees not reason to remove them to their Damage; but will allow them to be and remain with other Inhabitants that may be admitted into the Town to be there Setled; And that they have full Liberty when their Names and Number are determined to purchase of the few Indians there remaining for the Establishment of a Township accordingly.

Saving convenient Allotments and portions of Land to the remaining Indian Inhabitants for their Setling and Planting.

                                                         Is^t ADDINGTON Sec̃ry.

In the House of Representatives
Octo^r 23th 1713. Read

[Massachusetts Archives, cxiii. 600.]

The inhabitants of Groton had now become alarmed at the situation of affairs, fearing that the new town would take away some of their land. Through neglect the plan of the original grant, drawn up in the year 1668, had never been returned to the General Court for confirmation, as was customary in such cases; and this fact also excited further apprehension. It was not confirmed finally until February 10, 1717, several years after the incorporation of Nashobah.

NASHOBAH AND LITTLETON. 27

In the General Court Records (ix. 263) in the State Library, under the date of June 18, 1713, it is entered:—

Upon reading a Petition of the Inhabitants of the Town of Groton, Praying that the Return & Plat of the Surveyor of their Township impowered by the General Court may be Accepted for the Settlement & Ascertaining the Bounds of their Township, Apprehending they are likely to be prejudiced by a Survey lately taken of the Grant of Nashoba;

Voted a Concurrence with the Order pass'd thereon in the House of Represent[ves] That the Petitioners serve the Proprietors of Nashoba Lands with a copy of this Petition, That they may Shew Cause, if any they have on the second Fryday of the Session of this Court in the Fall of the Year, Why the Prayer therof may not be granted, & the Bounds of Groton settled according to the ancient Plat of said Town herewith exhibited.

There are two sets of General Court Records, — one in the State Library, and the other in the office of the Secretary of State, — sometimes varying slightly in phraseology; and I have quoted from the one or the other, as seemed best for my purpose, at the same time noting which one was used.

It is evident from the records that the Nashobah lands gave rise to much controversy. Many petitions were presented to the General Court, and many claims made, growing out of this territory. The following entry is found in the General Court Records (ix. 369) in the State Library, under the date of November 2, 1714:—

The following Order pass'd by the Represent[ves] Read & Concur'd; viz,

Upon Consideration of the many Petitions & Claims relating to the Land called Nashoba Land; Ordered that the said Nashoba Land be made a Township, with the Addition of such adjoining Lands of the Neighbouring Towns, whose Owners shall petition for that End, & that this Court should think fit to grant, That the said Nashoba Lands having been long since purchased of the Indians by M[r] Bulkley & Henchman one Half, the other Half by Whetcomb & Powers, That the said purchase be confirmed to the children of the said Bulkley, Whetcomb & Powers, & Cpt. Robert Meers as

Assignee to Mr Henchman according to their respective Proportions ; Reserving to the Inhabitants, who have settled within those Bounds, their Settlements with Divisions of Lands, in proportion to the Grantees, & such as shall be hereafter admitted ; the said Occupants or present Inhabitants paying in Proportion as others shall pay for their Allotments ;. Provided the said Plantation shall be settled with Thirty five Families & an orthodox Minister in three years time, And that Five hundred Acres of Land be reserved and laid out for the Benefit of any of the Descendants of the Indian Proprietors of the said Plantation, that may be surviving ; A Proportion thereof to be for Sarah Doublet alias Sarah Indian ;. The Rev. Mr John Leveret & Spencer Phips Esqr to be Trustees for the said Indians to take Care of the said reserved Lands for their Use. And it is further Ordered that Cpt. Hopestill Brown, Mr Timothy Wily & Mr Joseph Burnap of Reading be a Committee to lay out the said Five hundred Acres of Land reserved for the Indians, & to run the Line between Groton & Nashoba, at the Charge of both Parties & make Report to this Court, And that however the Line may divide the Land with regard to the Township, yet the Proprietors on either side may be continued in the Possession of their Improvements, paying as aforesaid ; And that no Persons legal Right or Property in the said Lands shall [be] hereby taken away or infringed.

       Consented to   J Dudley

 The report of this committee is entered in the same volume of General Court Records (ix. 395, 396) in which appears the order for their appointment. The date of October 20, mentioned in it, refers to the beginning of the session of the Legislature, which had been continued by several prorogations to that day.

 The following Report of the Committee for Running the Line between Groton & Nashoba Accepted by Represent^{ves} Read & Concur'd ; Viz.

 We the Subscribers appointed a Committee by the General Court to run the Line between Groton & Nashoba & to lay out Five hundred Acres of Land in said Nashoba to the the [*sic*] Descendants of the Indians ; Pursuant to said Order of Court, bearing Date

Octob' 20th [November 2?] 1714, We the Subscribers return as follows ;

That on the 30th of November last, we met on the Premises, & heard the Information of the Inhabitants of Groton, Nashoba & others of the Neighbouring Towns, referring to the Line that has been between Groton & Nashoba & seen several Records, out of Groton Town Book, & considered other Writings, that belong to Groton & Nashoba, & We have considered all, & We have run the Line (Which we account is the old Line between Groton & Nashoba ;) We began next Chelmsford Line, at a Heap of Stones, where, We were informed, that there had been a great Pine Tree, the Northeast Corner of Nashoba, and run Westerly by many old mark'd Trees, to a Pine Tree standing on the Southerly End of Brown Hill mark'd N and those marked Trees had been many times marked or renewed, thô they do not stand in a direct or strait Line to said Pine Tree on said Brown Hill ; And then from said Brown Hill we turned a little to the East of the South, & run to a white Oak being an old Mark, & so from said Oak to a Pitch Pine by a Meadow, being an other old Mark ; & the same Line extended to a white Oak near the North east Corner of Stow : And this is all, as we were informed, that Groton & Nashoba joins together : Notwithstanding the Committees Opinion is, that Groton Men be continued in their honest Rights, thô they fall within the Bounds of Nashoba ; And We have laid out to the Descendants of the Indians Five hundred Acres at the South east Corner of the Plantation of Nashoba ; East side, Three hundred Poles long, West side three hundred Poles, South & North ends, Two hundred & eighty Poles broad ; A large white Oak marked at the North west Corner, & many Line Trees we marked at the West side & North End, & it takes in Part of two Ponds.

Dated Decem! 14. 1714.

          HOPESTILL BROWN
          TIMOTHY WILY
          JOSEPH BURNAP

Consented to   J DUDLEY.

The incorporation of Nashobah on November 2, 1714, settled many of the disputes connected with the lands ; but on December 3 of the next year, the name was changed from Nashobah to Littleton. As already stated, the plan of the original Groton grant had never been returned by the proprietors to the General Court for confirmation; and this neglect had acted to their prejudice. After Littleton had been set off, the town of Groton undertook to repair the injury and make up the loss. John Shepley and John Ames were appointed agents to bring about the necessary confirmation by the General Court. It is an interesting fact to know that in their petition (General Court Records, x. 216, February 11, 1717, in the office of the Secretary of State) they speak of having in their possession at that time the original plan of the town, made by Danforth, in the year 1668, though it was somewhat defaced. In the language of the Records, it was said to be "with the Petitioner," which expression in the singular number may have been intentional, referring to John Shepley, probably the older one, as certainly the more influential, of the two agents. This plan was also exhibited before the General Court on June 18, 1713, according to the Records (ix. 263) of that date.

The case, as presented by the agents, was as follows: —

A petition of John Sheply & John Ames Agents for the Town of Groton Shewing that the General Assembly of the Province did in the year 1655, Grant unto Mr. Dean Winthrop & his Associates a Tract of Land of Eight miles quare for a Plantation to be called by the name of Groton, that Thom: & Jonathan Danforth did in the year 1668, lay out the said Grant, but the Plat thereof through Neglect was not returned to the Court for Confirmation that the said Plat thô something defaced is with the Petitioner, That in the Year 1713 Mr. Samuel Danforth Surveyour & Son of the abovesaid Jonathan Danforth, at the desire of the said Town of Groton did run the Lines & make an Implatment of the said Township laid out as before & found it agreeable to the former. Wh last Plat the Petitioners do herewith exhibit, And pray that this Honble Court would allow & confirm the same as the Township of Groton

In the House of Representves Feb. 10. 1717. Read, Read a second time, And Ordered that the Prayer of the Petition be so far granted that the Plat herewith exhibited (Althô not exactly conformable to the Original Grant of Eight Miles quare) be accounted, accepted & Confirmed as the Bounds of the Township of Groton in all parts,

Except where the said Township bounds on the Township of Littleton, Where the Bounds shall be & remain between the Towns as already stated & settled by this Court, And that this Order shall not be understood or interpreted to alter or infringe the Right & Title which any Inhabitant or Inhabitants of either of the said Towns have or ought to have to Lands in either of the said Townships

In Council, Read & Concur'd,
Consented to
SAM^{LL} SHUTE

[General Court Records (x. 216), February 11, 1717, in the office of the Secretary of State.]

III.

GROTON GORE AND THE PROVINCIAL LINE.

THE proprietors of Groton felt sore at the loss of their territory along the Nashobah line in the year 1714, though it would seem without reason. They had neglected to have the plan of their grant confirmed by the proper authorities at the proper time; and no one was to blame for this oversight but themselves. In the autumn of 1734 they represented to the General Court that in the laying out of the original plantation no allowance had been made for prior grants in the same territory, and that in settling the line with Littleton they had lost more than four thousand acres of land; and in consideration of these facts they petitioned for an unappropriated gore of land lying between Dunstable and Townsend.

The necessary steps for bringing the matter before the General Court at this time were taken at a town meeting, held on July 25, 1734. It was then stated that the town had lost more than twenty-seven hundred and eighty-eight acres by the encroachment of Littleton line; and that two farms had been laid out within the plantation before it was granted to the proprietors. Under these circumstances Benjamin Prescott was authorized to present the petition to the General Court, setting forth the true state of the case and all the facts connected with it. The two farms alluded to were Major Simon Willard's, situated at Nonacoicus, or Coicus, now within

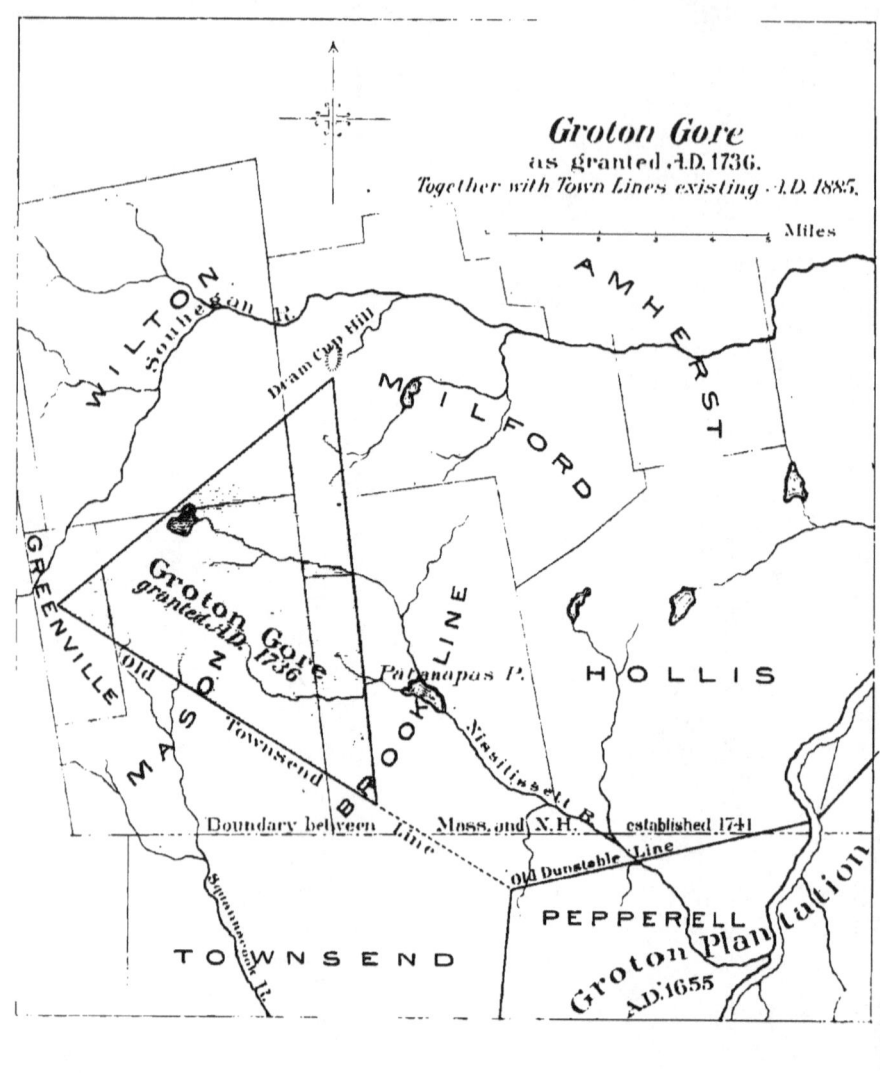

the limits of Ayer, and Ralph Reed's, in the neighborhood of the Ridges; so Mr. Butler told me several years before his death, giving Judge James Prescott as his authority, and I carefully wrote it down at the time. The statement is confirmed by the report of a committee on the petition of Josiah Sartell, made to the House of Representatives, on June 13, 1771. Willard's farm, however, was not laid out before the original plantation was granted, but in the spring of 1657, two years after the grant. At that time Danforth had not made his plan of the plantation, which fact may have given rise to the misapprehension. Ralph Reed was one of the original proprietors of the town, and owned a fifteen-acre right; but I do not find that any land was granted him by the General Court. Major Willard's farm comprised five hundred acres, according to the grant, but probably it was surveyed with the looseness and liberality of that period. Its shape can still be traced, in part, by the irregular boundary of the town of Ayer, along the western half of its southern border.

It has been incorrectly supposed, and more than once so stated in print, that the gore of land petitioned for by Benjamin Prescott lay in the territory now belonging to Pepperell; but this is a mistake. The only unappropriated land between Dunstable and Townsend, as asked for in the petition, lay in the angle made by the western boundary of Dunstable and the northern boundary of Townsend; and here it was granted. A reference to the accompanying map will show its situation; and furthermore it will throw a little light on Mr. Ithamar Bard Sawtelle's remark, in his History (page 50), that the town of Townsend had no northeast corner until the year 1741, when the new Provincial line was run. Before this time there had been some dispute in regard to the northeast corner, which was by no means well defined. At that period Dunstable was a very large township, and included within its territory several modern towns, lying mostly in New Hampshire. The manuscript records of the General Court define very clearly the lines of the Gore, and leave no doubt in regard to it. It lay within the present towns of Mason, Brookline,

Wilton, Milford, and Greenville, New Hampshire. Benjamin Prescott was at the time a member of the General Court, and the most influential man in town. His petition was presented to the House of Representatives on November 28, 1734, and referred to a committee, which made a report thereon a fortnight later. They are as follows: —

A Petition of *Benjamin Prescot*, Esq; Representative of the Town of *Groton*, and in behalf of the Proprietors of the said Town, shewing that the General Court in *May* 1655, in answer to the Petition of Mr. *Dean Winthrop* and others, were pleased to grant the Petitioners a tract of Land of the contents of eight miles square, the Plantation to be called *Groton*, that in taking a Plat of the said tract there was no allowance made for prior Grants &c. by means whereof and in settling the Line with *Littleton Anno* 1715, or thereabouts, the said Town of *Groton* falls short more than four thousand acres of the Original Grant, praying that the said Proprietors may obtain a Grant of what remains undisposed of of a Gore of Land lying between *Dunstable* and *Townshend*, or an equivalent elsewhere of the Province Land. Read and *Ordered*, That Col. *Chandler*, Capt. *Blanchard*, Capt. *Hobson*, Major *Epes*, and Mr. *Hale*, be a Committee to take this Petition under consideration, and report what may be proper for the Court to do in answer thereto.

[Journal of the House of Representatives (page 94), November 28, 1734.]

Col. *Chandler* from the Committee appointed the 28*th*. ult. to consider the Petition of *Benjamin Prescot*, Esq; in behalf of the Proprietors of *Groton*, made report, which was read and accepted, and in answer to this Petition, *Voted*, That a Grant of ten thousand eight hundred acres of the Lands lying in the *Gore* between *Dunstable* and *Townshend*, be and hereby is made to the Proprietors of the Town of *Groton*, as an equivalent for what was taken from them by *Littleton* and *Coyachus* or *Willard's Farm* (being about two acres and a half for one) and is in full satisfaction thereof, and that the said Proprietors be and hereby are allowed and impowred by a Surveyor and Chain-men on Oath to survey and lay out the said ten thousand eight hundred acres in the said *Gore*, and return a Plat thereof to this Court within twelve months for confirmation to them their heirs and assigns respectively.

Sent up for Concurrence.

[Journal of the House of Representatives (page 119), December 12, 1734.]

GROTON GORE AND THE PROVINCIAL LINE. 35

The proprietors of Groton had a year's time allowed them, in which they could lay out the grant, but they appear to have taken fifteen months for the purpose. The record of the grant is as follows:—

A Memorial of Benj^a Prescott Esq: Represent^a of the Town of Groton in behalf of the Proprietors there, praying that the Votes of the House on his Memorial & a plat of Ten Thousand Eight hundred Acres of Land, lately Granted to the said Proprietors, as Entred in the House the 25 of March last, may be Revived and Granted, The bounds of which Tract of Land as Mentioned on the said Plat are as follows vizt; begining at the North West Corner of Dunstable at Dram Cup hill by Sohegan River and Runing South in Dunstable line last Perambulated and Run by a Com^{tee} of the General Court, two Thousand one hundred & fifty two poles to Townshend line, there making an angle, and Runing West 31 1-2 Deg. North on Townshend line & province Land Two Thousand and Fifty Six poles to a Pillar of Stones then turning and Runing by Province Land 31 1-2 deg North two Thousand & forty Eight poles to Dunstable Corner first mentioned

In the House of Represent^s Read & Ordered that the prayer of the Memorial be Granted, and further that the within Plat as Reformed and Altered by Jonas Houghton Survey^r be and hereby is accepted and the Lands therein Delineated and Described (Excepting the said One Thousand Acres belonging to Cambridge School Farm and therein included) be and hereby are Confirmed to the Proprietors of the Town of Groton their heirs and Assignes Respectivly forever, According to their Several Interests; Provided the same do not interfere with any former Grant of this Court nor Exceeds the Quantity of Eleven thousand and Eight hundred Acres and the Committee for the Town of Ipswich are Allowed and Impowred to lay out such quantity of Land on their West line as is Equivalent to what is taken off their East line as aforesaid, and Return a plat thereof to this Court within twelve Months for confirmation. In Council Read & Concurr'd.

Consented to   J Belcher

And in Answer to the said Memorial of Benj^a Prescott Esqr
In the House of Represent^s Ordered that the prayer of the Memorial be Granted and the Com^{tee} for the new Township Granted

to some of the Inhabitants of Ipswich are hereby Allowed to lay out an Equivalent on the West line of the said New Township Accordingly

In Council Read & Concurr'd

       Consented to   J BELCHER

[General Court Records (xvi. 334), June 15, 1736, in the office of the Secretary of State.]

This grant, now made to the proprietors of Groton, interfered with the territory previously given in April, 1735, to certain inhabitants of Ipswich; but the mistake was soon rectified, as appears by the following: —

Voted, That one thousand seven hundred Acres of the unappropriated Lands of the Province be and hereby is given and granted to the Proprietors or Grantees of the Township lately granted to sixty Inhabitants of the Town of *Ipswich*, as an Equivalent for about that quantity being taken off their Plat by the Proprietors of the Common Lands of *Groton*, and that the *Ipswich* Grantees be allowed to lay out the same on the Northern or Westerly Line of the said new Township or on both sides.

       Sent up for Concurrence.

[Journal of the House of Representatives (page 108), January 12, 1736.]

The record of the grant clearly marks the boundaries of Groton Gore, and by it they can easily be identified. Dram Cup Hill, near Souhegan River, the old northwest corner of Dunstable, is in the present town of Milford, New Hampshire. From that hill the line ran south for six or seven miles, following the western boundary of Dunstable, until it came to the old Townsend line; then it turned and ran northwesterly six miles or more, when turning again it made for the original starting-place at Dunstable northwest corner. These lines enclosed a triangular district which became known as Groton Gore; in fact, the word *gore* means a lot of land of triangular shape. This territory is now entirely within the State of New Hampshire, lying mostly in Mason, but partly in Brookline, Wilton, Milford, and Greenville. It touches in no place the tract, hitherto erroneously supposed to comprise the Gore.

It was destined, however, to remain only a few years in the possession of the proprietors; but during this short period it was used by them for pasturing cattle. Mr. John Boynton Hill, in his History of the Town of Mason, New Hampshire, says : —

Under this grant, the inhabitants of Groton took possession of, and occupied the territory. It was their custom to cut the hay upon the meadows, and stack it, and early in the spring to send up their young cattle to be fed upon the hay, under the care of Boad, the negro slave. They would cause the woods to be fired, as it was called, that is, burnt over in the spring; after which fresh and succulent herbage springing up, furnished good store of the finest feed, upon which the cattle would thrive and fatten through the season. Boad's camp was upon the east side of the meadow, near the residence of the late Joel Ames. (Page 26.)

In connection with the loss of the gore, a brief statement of the boundary question between Massachusetts and New Hampshire is here given.

During many years the dividing line between these two Provinces was the subject of controversy. The cause of dispute dated back to the time when the original grant was made to the Colony of Massachusetts Bay. The charter was drawn up in England at a period when little was known in regard to the interior of this country; and the boundary lines, necessarily, were somewhat indefinite. The Merrimack River was an important factor in fixing the limits of the grant, as the northern boundary of Massachusetts was to be a line three miles north of any and every part of it. At the date of the charter, the general direction of the river was not known, but it was incorrectly assumed to be easterly and westerly. As a matter of fact, the course of the Merrimack is southerly, for a long distance from where it is formed by the union of the Winnepesaukee and the Pemigewasset Rivers, and then it turns and runs twenty-five or thirty miles in a northeasterly direction to its mouth; and this deflexion in the current caused the dispute. The difference between the actual and the supposed direction was a matter of little practical importance so long as the neighboring territory remained unsettled, or so long as the two Provinces were essentially under one government; but as the population increased it became an exciting and vexatious question. Towns were chartered by Massachusetts in territory claimed by New Hampshire, and this action led to bitter feeling and provoking legislation. Massachusetts contended for the land "nominated in the bond," which would carry the line fifty miles northward into the very heart of New Hampshire; and on the other hand that Province strenuously opposed this view of the case, and claimed that the line should run, east and west, three miles north of the mouth of the river. At one time, a royal commission was appointed to consider the subject, but their labors produced no satisfactory result. At last the matter was carried to England for a decision, which was rendered by the king on March 5, 1739-40. His judgment was final, and in favor of New Hampshire. It gave that Province not only all the territory in dispute, but a strip of land fourteen miles in width, lying along her southern border, mostly west of the Merrimack, which she had never claimed. This strip was the tract of land between the line running east and west, three miles north of the southernmost trend of the river, and a similar line three miles north of its mouth. By the decision twenty-eight townships were taken from Massachusetts and transferred to New Hampshire. The settlement of this disputed question was undoubtedly a public benefit, although it caused, at the time, a great deal of hard feeling. In establishing the new boundary, Pawtucket Falls, situated now in the city of Lowell, and near the most southern portion of the river's course, was taken as the starting-place; and the line which now separates the two States was run west, three miles north of this point. It was surveyed officially in the spring of 1741, with reference to the settlement of this dispute.

The new boundary passed through the original Groton Plantation, cutting off a triangular portion of its territory, now within the limits of Nashua, and a very small corner of

Hollis, and went to the southward of Groton Gore, leaving that tract of land wholly in New Hampshire.

On June 3, 1771, thirty years after the Gore had been lost by the running of the Provincial line, the proprietors of the town held a meeting, and appointed Lieutenant Josiah Sawtell, Colonel John Bulkley, and Lieutenant Nathaniel Parker a committee to petition the General Court for a grant of land to make up for this loss. They presented the matter to that body on June 7, and the following entry in the records gives the result : —

> The Committee on the Petition of *Josiah Sartel*, and others, reported.
>
> Read and accepted, and *Whereas it appears to this Court, That the Proprietors aforesaid, had a Grant made to them by the General Court in* April 1735, *of Ten Thousand, Eight Hundred Acres of Land, in Consideration of Land taken from said* Groton *by* Littleton, *Major* Willard *and* Read's *Farms being prior Grants, and for their extraordinary Suffering in the former Indian Wars ; and in* June 1736 *said Grant was confirmed to said Proprietors, since which Time, the said Proprietors have been entirely dispossessed of said Land by the running of the Line between this Province and* New-Hampshire : *And whereas it appears there has been no Compensation made to the said Proprietors of* Groton, *for the Lands lost as aforesaid, excepting Three Thousand Acres granted in* November *last,* to James Prescot, William Prescot, *and* Oliver Prescot *for their Proportion thereof.* Therefore *Resolved,* That in Lieu thereof, there be granted to the Proprietors of *Groton,* their Heirs and Assigns forever, Seven Thousand and Eight Hundred Acres of the unappropriated Lands belonging to this Province, in the Western Part of the Province, to be layed out adjoining to some former Grant, and that they return a Plan thereof, taken by a Surveyor and Chainmen under Oath into the Secretary's Office, within twelve Months for Confirmation.
>
> Sent up for Concurrence.
>
> [Journal of the House of Representatives (page 44), June 13, 1771.]

These conditions, as recommended by the report of the committee, appear to have been fulfilled, and a grant was accordingly made. It lay on the eastern border of Berkshire

County, just south of the central part, and was described as follows: —

The Committee on a Plan of a Tract of Land granted to the Proprietors of *Groton*, reported.

Read and accepted, and *Resolved*, That the Plan hereunto annexed, containing three Thousand nine Hundred and sixty Acres of Province Land, laid out in Part to satisfy a Grant made by the Great and General Court at their Sessions in *June* 1771, to the Proprietors of Groton, in Lieu of Land they lost by the late running of the *New-Hampshire* Line, as mention'd in their Petition, laid out in the County of *Berkshire*, and is bounded as followeth, viz. Beginning at a Burch Tree and Stones laid round it the Southwest Corner of *Tyringham-Equivalent* Lands standing on the East Branch of *Farmington* River; then North eighteen Degrees East in the West Line of said *Equivalent* five Hundred and sixty-one Rods to a small Beach Tree and Stones laid round it, which Tree is the Southeast Corner of a Grant of Land called *Woolcut's* Grant; then running West eighteen Degrees North in the South Line of said Grant two Hundred and forty Rods to a Beach Tree marked I. W. and Stones laid round it, which is the Southwest Corner of said Grant; then running North eighteen Degrees East in the West Line of said Grant four Hundred Rods to a Heap of Stones which is the Northwest Corner of said Grant; then running East eighteen Degrees South two Hundred and forty Rods in the North Line of said Grant to a large Hemlock Tree and Stones laid round it, which is the Northeast Corner of said Grant; it is also the Northwest Corner of said *Equivalent*, and the Southwest Corner of a Grant called *Taylor's* Grant; then running North eighteen Degrees East one Hundred and sixty Rods in the West Line of said *Taylor's* Grant to the Northwest Corner of the same; then running East nine Degrees South in the Line of said *Taylor's* Grant eight Hundred Rods to a Stake and Stones standing in the West Line of *Blanford*, marked W. T. then running North eighteen Degrees East in said *Blanford* West Line five Hundred and thirty Rods to a Beach Tree and Stones laid round it which is the Northwest Corner of said *Blanford;* then running East ten Degrees South forty-two Rods in the North Line of said *Blanford* to a Stake and Stones which is the Southwest Corner of *Merryfield;* then running North ten Degrees East in said *Merryfield* West Line three Hundred and three Rods to a Heap of

Stones the Southeast Corner of *Becket;* then running West two Degrees South in said *Becket* South Line four Hundred and twenty-six Rods to the Northeast Corner of a Grant of Land called *Belcher's* Grant; then running South in the East Line of said *Belcher's* Grant two Hundred and sixteen Rods to a small Maple Tree marked T. R, which is the Northwest Corner of a Grant of Land called *Rand's* Grant; then running East in the North Line of said *Rand's* Grant two Hundred and fifty Rods to a Hemlock Pole and Stones laid round it, which is the Northeast Corner of said *Rand's* Grant; then running South in the East Line of said *Rand's* Grant three Hundred and thirty-one Rods to a Hemlock Tree marked and Stones laid round it, which is the Southeast Corner of said *Rand's* Grant; then running West in the South Line of said *Rand's* Grant two Hundred and fifty Rods to a Beach Pole marked T. R. the Southwest Corner of said *Rand's* Grant; then running North in the West Line of said *Rand's* Grant eighty-three Rods to the Southeast Corner of said *Belcher's* Grant; then running West bounding North three Hundred and forty-eight on said *Belcher's* Grant and four Hundred and fifty-three Rods on a Grant called *Chandler's* Grant, then running North on the West Line of said *Chandler's* Grant four Hundred and sixty to said *Becket's* South Line; then running West in said *Becket* South Line twenty Rods to a Stake and Stones the North West Corner of additional Lands belonging to the Four *Housatonick* Townships; then running South two Degrees West one Thousand four Hundred and eighty-eight Rods in the East Line of said additional Lands to the Place where the said East Line crosses said *Farmington* River; then Southerly or down Stream three Hundred and thirty Rods to the first Bounds, bounding Westerly on said River, be accepted, and is hereby accepted and confirmed unto the Proprietors of *Groton* aforesaid, their Heirs and Assigns forever. *Provided* the same doth not exceed the Quantity aforementioned, nor interfere with any former Grant.

Sent up for Concurrence.

[Journal of the House of Representatives (pages 182, 183), April 24, 1772.]

I am unable to say how or when this territory was disposed of by the proprietors. Seven or eight years before this time, James, William, and Oliver Prescott, acting for themselves as extensive owners, had petitioned the General Court for a tract of land to make up their own losses. They were the sons of the Honorable Benjamin Prescott, through whose influence and agency the original Groton Gore was granted, and they were also the largest proprietors of the town. The following extracts from the Journal of the House relate to their application : —

A Petition of *James Prescot*, and others, Children and Heirs of *Benjamin Prescot*, late of *Groton*, Esq ; deceased, praying a Grant of the unappropriated Lands of this Province, in consideration of sundry Tracts which they have lost by the late running of the Line between this Government and *New-Hampshire*.

Read and committed to Col. *Clap*, Col. *Nickols*, Col. *Williams* of *Roxbury*, Col. *Buckminster*, and Mr. *Lancaster*, to consider and Report.

[Journal of the House of Representatives (page 187), January 12, 1764.]

On February 3, 1764, this petition was put over to the May session, though I do not find that it came up then for consideration. It does not appear again for some years.

A Petition of *James Prescot*, Esq ; and others, praying that a Grant of Land may be made them in Lieu of a former Grant, which falls within the *New-Hampshire* Line.

[Journal of the House of Representatives (page 129), November 2, 1770.]

This petition was referred to a committee consisting of Dr. Samuel Holten, of Danvers, Colonel Joseph Gerrish, of Newbury, and Mr. Joshua Bigelow, of Worcester.

The Committee on the Petition of *James Prescot*, Esq ; and others, reported.

Read and accepted, and *Resolved*, That in Lieu of Lands mentioned in the Petition, there be granted to the Petitioners, their Heirs and Assigns, Four Thousand Four Hundred Acres of the unappropriated Lands belonging to the Province, to be laid out in the Westerly Part thereof, adjoining to some former Grants, provided they can find the same ; or Five Thousand Eight Hundred and Eighty Acres of the unappropriated Lands lying on the Easterly side of *Saco* River; it being their Proportion in said Grant: And return a Plan thereof taken by a Surveyor and Chainmen under Oath, into the Secretary's Office within Twelve Months.

Sent up for Concurrence.

[Journal of the House of Representatives (page 156), November 14, 1770.]

The Committee appointed to consider the Plan of two Tracts of Land granted to *James Prescot*, Esq; and others, reported.

Read and accepted. *Resolved*, That both the above Plans, the one containing Four Thousand one Hundred and thirty Acres, the other containing two Hundred and seventy Acres, delineated and described as is set forth by the Surveyor in the Description thereof hereunto annexed, be accepted, and hereby is confirmed to *James Prescot*, Esq; and others named in their Petition, and to their Heirs and Assigns in Lieu of and full Satisfaction for Four Thousand four Hundred Acres of Land lost by the late running of the Line between this Province and *New-Hampshire*, as mention'd in a Grant made by both Houses of the Assembly, A. D. 1765, but not consented to by the Governor. *Provided* both said Plans together do not exceed the Quantity of Four Thousand four Hundred Acres, nor interfere with any former Grant.

Sent up for Concurrence.

[Journal of the House of Representatives (pages 73, 74), June 22, 1771.]

It is evident from these reports that the Prescott brothers took the forty-four hundred acres in the westerly part of the Province, rather than the fifty-eight hundred and eighty acres on the easterly side of the Saco River, though I have been unable to identify, beyond a doubt, the tract of land thus granted. Perhaps the smaller parcel was the one mentioned in the Memorial of the One Hundredth Anniversary of the Incorporation of Middlefield, Massachusetts, August 15, 1883. The town is situated on the westerly border of Hampshire County, forming a jog into Berkshire, and was made up in part of Prescott's grant. A map is given in the "Memorial" volume (page 16) which shows that the grant was originally in Berkshire County, very near the tract of land given to the proprietors of Groton.

Professor Edward Payson Smith, of Worcester, delivered an historical address on the occasion of the anniversary, and he says : —

Prescott's Grant, the nucleus of the town, appears as a large quadrilateral, containing more than a thousand acres in the north and west part of the town. Who the Prescott was to whom the grant was made is not known, further than that he must have been some one who had rendered military or other services to the State. That he was the Prescott who commanded at Bunker Hill is, indeed, possible ; but, as the grant was probably made before the Revolutionary War, that supposition seems hardly tenable. (Page 15.)

IV.

WESTFORD AND HARVARD.

of 1730

IN the early autumn, the original plantation had suffered further dismemberment, when a slice of its territory was given to Westford. It was a long and narrow tract of land, triangular in shape, with its base resting on Stony Brook Pond, now known as Forge Pond, and coming to a point near Millstone Hill, where the boundary lines of Groton, Westford, and Tyngsborough intersect. The Reverend Edwin Ruthven Hodgman, in his History of Westford, says:—

Probably there was no computation of the area of this triangle at any time. Only four men are named as the owners of it, but they, it is supposed, held titles to only a portion, and the remainder was wild, or "common," land. (Page 25.)

In the Journal of the House of Representatives (page 9), September 10, 1730, there is recorded, in connection with this transfer of territory,—

A Petition of *Jonas Prescot, Ebenezer Prescot, Abner Kent*, and *Ebenezer Townsend*, Inhabitants of the Town of *Groton*, praying, That they and their Estates, contained in the following Boundaries, *viz.* beginning at the *Northwesterly* Corner of *Stony Brook* Pond, from thence extending to the *Northwesterly* Corner of *Westford*, commonly called *Tyng*'s Corner, and so bound *Southerly* by said Pond, may be set off to the Town of *Westford*, for Reasons mentioned. Read and *Ordered*, That the Petitioners within named, with their Estates, according to the Bounds before recited, be and hereby are to all Intents and Purposes set off from the Town of *Groton*, and annexed to the said Town of *Westford*.

Sent up for Concurrence.

This order received the concurrence of the Council, and was signed by the Governor, on the same day that it passed the House.

During this period the town of Harvard was incorporated. It was made up from portions of Groton, Lancaster, and Stow, and the engrossed Act signed by the Governor, on June 29, 1732. The petition for the township was presented to the General Court nearly two years before the date of incorporation. In the Journal of the House of Representatives (pages 84, 85), October 9, 1730, it is recorded:—

A Petition of *Jonas Houghton, Simon Stone, Jonathan Whitney*, and *Thomas Wheeler*, on behalf of themselves, and on behalf and at the desire of sundry of the Inhabitants on the extream parts of the Towns of *Lancaster, Groton* and *Stow*, named in the Schedule thereunto annexed; praying, That a Tract of Land (with the Inhabitants thereon, particularly described and bounded in said Petition) belonging to the Towns above-mentioned, may be incorporated and erected into a distinct Township, agreeable to said Bounds, for Reasons mentioned. Read, together with the said Schedule, and *Ordered*, That the Petitioners serve the Towns of *Lancaster, Groton* and *Stow* with Copies of the Petition, that they may shew Cause (if any they have) on the first Thursday of the next Session, why the Prayer thereof may not be granted.

Sent up for Concurrence.

Further on, in the same Journal (page 136), December 29, 1730, it is also recorded:—

The Petition of *Jonas Houghton, Simon Stone*, and others, praying as entred the 9th. of *October* last. Read again, together with the Answers of the Towns of *Lancaster, Groton* and Stow, and *Ordered*, That Maj. *Brattle* and Mr. *Samuel Chandler*, with such as the Honourable Board shall appoint, be a Committee, (at the Charge of the Petitioners) to repair to the Land Petitioned for to

be a Township, that they carefully view and consider the Situation and Circumstances of the Petitioners, and Report their Opinion what may be proper for this Court to do in Answer thereto, at their next Session.
Sent up for Concurrence.

Ebenezer Burrel Esq ; brought down from the Honourable Board, the Report of the Committee appointed by this Court the 30th of *December* last, to take under Consideration the Petition of *Jonas Houghton* and others, in behalf of themselves and sundry of the Inhabitants of the *Eastern* part of the Towns of *Lancaster*, *Groton* and *Stow*, praying that they may be erected into a separate Township. Likewise a Petition of *Jacob Houghton* and others, of the *North-easterly* part of the Town of *Lancaster*, praying the like. As also a Petition of sundry of the Inhabitants of the *South-west* part of the *North-east* Quarter of the Township of *Lancaster*, praying they may be continued as they are. Pass'd in Council, *viz.* In Council, *June* 21, 1731. Read, and *Ordered*, That this Report be accepted.

Sent down for Concurrence. Read and Concurred.

[Journal of the House of Representatives (page 52), June 22, 1731.]

The original copy of the petition for Harvard is now lost; but in the first volume (page 53) of "Ancient Plans Grants &c." among the Massachusetts Archives, there is a rough plan of the town, with a list of the petitioners, which may be the "Schedule" referred to in the extract from the printed Journal. It appears from this document that, in forming the new town, forty-eight hundred and thirty acres of land were taken from the territory of Groton; and with the tract were nine families, including six by the name of Farnsworth. This region comprised the district known, even now, as the Old Mill, where Jonas Prescott had, as early as the year 1667, a mill for grinding and sawing. The heads of these families were Jonathan Farnsworth, Eleazer Robbins, Simon Stone, Jr., Jonathan Farnsworth, Jr., Jeremiah Farnsworth, Eleazer Davis, Ephraim Farnsworth, Reuben Farnsworth, and Daniel Farnsworth, who had petitioned the General Court to be set off from Groton. On this plan of Harvard the names of John

Burk, John Burk, Jr., and John Davis, appear in opposition to Houghton's petition. Statistics also are given relating to Lancaster and Stow.

Eleazer Davis, one of the petitioners, was in the famous Lovewell's Fight, on May 8, 1725, at Pequawket, now within the limits of Fryeburg, Maine. In the Journal of the House of Representatives (page 42), June 15, 1738, is entered: —

A Petition of *Eleazer Davis* of *Harvard* in the County of *Worcester*, praying the Consideration of the Court on Account of his Sufferings and Services, particularly the Wounds and Smart received in the Fight under the Command of the late Capt. *Lovewell*, against the Indian Enemy at *Pigwacket*.

Read and *Ordered*, That *John Russell*, and *Robert Hale*, Esqrs; Mr. *Moodey*, and Mr. *Terry*, be a Committee to consider the said Petition, and report what may be proper to be done thereon.

On the following day Mr. Russell, the chairman of the Committee, reported an order that —

The Sum of *four Pounds* per Annum of the new tenor Bills, be granted and allowed to be paid out of the publick Treasury for the space of five Years to the Petitioner *Eleazer Davis*, to commence from the first Day of this Instant *June*, by way of Stipend or Pension, on Account of the Wounds and Smart received as within mentioned.

Sent up for concurrence.

Another paper relating to the town of Harvard is the following memorial, which is, without doubt, substantially the same as the original petition, now lost: —

To his Excellency Jonathan Belcher Esq! Cap! General and Governour in Chief The Hon!!e The Council and the Honourable House of Representatives of His Majestys Province of the Massachusetts Bay in New England in General Court Assembled by Adjournment Decemb! 16 1730

The Memorial of Jonas Haughton Simon Stone Jonathan Whitney and Thomas Wheeler Humbly Sheweth

That upon their Petition to this Great and Honourable Court in October last [the 9th] praying that a Certain Tract of Land belonging to Lancaster Stow and Groton with the Inhabitants thereon may be Erected into a Distinct and Seperate Township (and for Reasons therein Assigned) your Excellency and Honours were pleased to Order that the petitioners Serve The Towns of Lancaster Groton and Stow with a Copy of their said Petition that they may shew Cause if any they have on the first Thursday of the next Sessions why the prayers thereof may not be granted

And for as much as this great and Honble Court now Sitts by Adjournment and the next Session may be very Remote And your Memorialists have attended the Order of this Honble Court in serving the said Several Towns with Copys of the said Petition And the partys are now attending and Desirous the hearing thereon may be brought forward ye former order of this Hon^l Court notwithstanding

They therefore most humbly pray your Excellency & Honours would be pleased to Cause the hearing to be had this present Session and that a Certain day may be assigned for the same as your Excellency & Honours in your great wisdom & Justice shall see meet.

And your Memorialists as in Duty bound Shall Ever pray

JONAS HOUGHTON
SIMON STOON Juner
JONATHAN WHITNEY
THOMAS WHELER

In the House of Rep^{tives} Decr 17 1730 Read and in Answer to this Petition Ordered That the Pet^{rs} give Notice to the Towns of Lancaster Groton and Stow or their Agents that they give in their Answer on the twenty ninth Inst^t why the Prayer of the Petition within referred to may not be granted

Sent up for Concurrence

J QUINCY Sp^{kr}

In Council Dec. 18, 1730; Read and Concur'd

J WILLARD Sec̃ry

[Massachusetts Archives, cxiv. 6–8.]

In the Journal of the House of Representatives (page 45) June 29, 1732, the following entry is made:—

A Bill Entitled *An Act for erecting a new Town within the County of* Worcester *by the Name of* Harvard.

By this Act the town was incorporated, and so named in honor of the founder of Harvard College, probably at the suggestion of Jonathan Belcher, Governor of the Province at that time, and a graduate of the college. The engrossed Act on parchment is still preserved in the office of the Secretary of State, and the following is a copy. It will be noticed, however, that the name of the town is left blank, except in the title, where it was written by Secretary Willard. It was not unusual in this kind of legislation at that period to leave the name of a town blank in the Act of Incorporation, when it passed the General Court; and subsequently it was filled in by the Governor, or at his order:—

Anno Regni Regis Georgii Secundi Quinto & Sexto

An Act for erecting a New Town within the county of Worcester, by the name of Harvard

Whereas the Inhabitants of the extream parts of the Towns of Lancaster Groton and Stow have laboured under much difficulty and inconvenience by reason of their remoteness from the places of publick Worship in the Towns to which they respectively belong, & have supported the Cost and Charge of preaching among them for several years past without any Consideration from their Towns, and have addressed this Court for Relief, & that they may be set off a distinct township by themselves

Be it therefore Enacted by His Excellency the Governour, Council and Representatives in General Court assembled & by the authority of the same that the Lands in the extream parts of the Towns of Lancaster Groton and Stow as the same are hereafter bounded and described be and hereby are Set off, & Constituted a seperate & distinct Township by the name of Harvard viz! begining at the Southerly End of the Causeway, near the House of Samuel Wilson in Lancaster and from thence running North West and by West till the line meets with Lancaster [Nashua] River, & from said Cause Way running South East & by East to Lancaster East bounds then running Northerly in the East Bounds of Lancaster till it comes to Beaver Brook, then bounding on said Brook till it comes to Littleton Bounds, and then running on said Littleton line near to the Northwest corner thereof vizt. so far as that a West North West

Line shall leave the dwelling house of James Stone in Groton six perch to the Northward, and continuing the same Course to Lancaster River aforesaid, excepting Coyacus ffarm or so much thereof as shall fall within the bounds above said; and to bound West on said River and that the Inhabitants of the said lands as before bounded and described be and hereby are vested with all the powers privileges and Immunities which the Inhabitants of any Town in this province are or by Law ought to be vested with

provided that the ffreeholders and other Inhabitants of the said Town Settle a learned and Orthodox Minister among them within the space of two years and also erect an House for the publick Worship of God

and Be it further Enacted by the Authority aforesaid that the aforesaid Town of   be and hereby is Declared to be within the County of Worcester, Any Law Usage or Custom to the contrary notwithstanding

 1732 June 20th. This Bill having been read three several times in the House of Representatives passed to be Enacted

 1732 June 21st   J Quincy Spkr

 1732 June 29 This Bill having been read three several Times in Council passed to be Enacted   J Willard Secry

By His Excellency the Governr
June 29, 1732 I consent to the Enacting of this Bill
                 J Belcher

The next dismemberment of the Groton grant took place in the winter of 1738-39, when a parcel of land was set off to Littleton. I do not find a copy of the petition for this change, but from Mr. Sartell's communication it seems to have received the qualified assent of the town:—

To his Excellency Jonathan Belcher Esqr Captain General & Governour in Chief &c the Honorable Council and House of Representatives in General Court assembled at Boston Jany 1, 1738.

May it please your Excellency and the Honorable Court

Whereas there is Petition offered to your Excellency and the Honorable Court by several of the Inhabitants of the Town of Groton praying to be annexed to the Town of Littleton &c

The Subscriber as Representative of said Town of Groton and in Behalf of said Town doth hereby manifest the Willingness of the Inhabitants of Groton in general that the petitioners should be annexed to the said Town of Littleton with the Lands that belong to them Lying within the Line Petitioned for, but there being a Considerable Quantity of Proprietors Lands and other particular persons Lying within the Line that is Petitioned for by the said Petitioners. The Subscriber in Behalf of said Town of Groton & the Proprietors and others would humbly pray your Excellency and the Honorable Court that that part of their Petition may be rejected if in your Wisdom you shall think it proper and that they be sett off with the lands only that belong to them Lying within the Line Petitioned for as aforesaid, and the Subscriber in Behalf of the Town of Groton &c will as in Duty Bound ever pray &c

NATHANIEL SARTELL

[Massachusetts Archives, cxiv. 300.]

John Jeffries, Esq; brought down the Petition of *Peter Lawrence* and others of *Groton*, praying to be annexed to *Littleton*, as entred the 12th ult. Pass'd in Council, *viz.* In Council *January 4th* 1738. Read again, together with the Answer of *Nathanael Sartell*, Esq; Representative for the Town of *Groton*, which being considered, *Ordered*, That the Prayer of the Petition be so far granted as that the Petitioners with their Families & Estates within the Bounds mentioned in the Petition be and hereby are set off from the Town of *Groton*, and are annexed to and accounted as part of the Town of *Littleton*, there to do Duty and receive Priviledge accordingly.

Sent down for Concurrence. Read and concur'd.

[Journal of the House of Representatives (page 86), January 4, 1738.]

V.

DUNSTABLE, HOLLIS, AND NOTTINGHAM.

I.

In the autumn of 1738, many of the settlers living in the northerly part of Groton, now within the limits of Pepperell, and in the westerly part of Dunstable, now Hollis, New Hampshire, were desirous to be set off in a new township. Their petition for this object was also signed by a considerable number of non-resident proprietors, and duly presented to the General Court. The reasons given by them for the change are found in the following documents: —

To His Excellency Jon.^a Belcher Esqr Captain General and Governour in Chief &c The Honble the Council and House of Rep^{tives} in General Court Assembled at Boston November the 29th 1738

The Petition of the Subscribers Inhabitants and Proprietors of the Towns of Dunstable and Groton.

Humbly Sheweth

That your Petitioners are Situated on the Westerly side Dunstable Township and the Northerly side Groton Township those in the Township of Dunstable in General their houses are nine or ten miles from Dunstable Meeting house and those in the Township of Groton none but what lives at least on or near Six miles from Groton Meeting house by which means your petitioners are deprived of the benefit of preaching, the greatest part of the year, nor is it possible at any season of the year for their familys in General to get to

Meeting under which Disadvantages your pet[rs]. has this Several years Laboured, excepting the Winter Seasons for this two winters past, which they have at their Own Cost and Charge hired preaching amongst themselves which Disadvantages has very much prevented peoples Settling land there.

That there is a Tract of good land well Situated for a Township of the Contents of about Six miles and an half Square bounded thus, beginning at Dunstable Line by Nashaway River So running by the Westerly side said River Southerly One mile in Groton Land, then running Westerly a Paralel Line with Groton North Line, till it comes to Townsend Line and then turning and running north to Grotton Northwest Corner, and from Grotton Northwest Corner by Townsend line and by the line of Groton New Grant till it comes to be five miles and an half to the Northward of Groton North Line from thence due east, Seven miles, from thence South to Nashua River and So by Nashua River Southwesterly to Grotton line the first mentioned bounds, which described Lands can by no means be prejudicial either to the Town of Dunstable or Groton (if not coming within Six miles or thereabouts of either of their Meeting houses at the nearest place) to be taken off from them and Erected into a Seperate Township.

That there is already Settled in the bounds of the aforedescribed Tract near forty familys and many more ready to come on were it not for the difficulties and hardships afores[d]. of getting to Meeting. These with many other disadvantages We find very troublesome to Us, Our living so remote from the Towns We respectively belong to.

Wherefore your Petitioners most humbly pray Your Excellency and Honours would take the premises into your Consideration and make an Act for the Erecting the aforesaid Lands into a Seperate and distinct Township with the powers priviledges and Immunities of a distinct and Seperate Township under such restrictions and Limitations, as you in your Great Wisdom shall see meet.

And Whereas it will be a great benefit and Advantage to the Non resident proprietors owning Lands there by Increasing the Value of their Lands or rendering easy Settleing the same, Your Pet[rs]. also pray that they may be at their proportionable part according to their respective Interest in Lands there, for the building a Meeting house and Settling a Minister, and so much towards Constant preaching as in your wisdom shall be thought proper.

Settlers on the afores.ᵈ Lands

Obadiah Parker	Peter Wheeler
Josiah Blood	Robert Colburn
Jerahmal Cumings	David Vering
Eben.ʳ Pearce	Philip Woolerick
Will.ᵐ Colburn	Nath.ˡ Blood
Stephen Harris	William Adams
Tho.ˢ Dinsmoor	Joseph Taylor
Peter Pawer	Moses Procter
Abr.ᵐ Taylor Jun.ʳ	Will.ᵐ Shattuck
Benj.ⁿ Farley	Tho.ˢ Navins
Henry Barton	

Non Resident Proprietors

Samuel Browne	Sam.ˡ Baldwin
W Browne	Daniel Remant
Joseph Blanchard	John Malven
John Fowle Jun.ʳ	Jon.ᵃ Malven
Nath Saltonstall	James Cumings
Joseph Eaton	Isaac Farwell
Joseph Lemmon	Eben.ʳ Procter
Jeremiah Baldwin	

In the House of Representatives Dec.ʳ 12.ᵗʰ 1738. Read and Ordered that the Petitioners Serve the Towns of Grotton and Dunstable with Coppys of the petition

In Council January 4.ᵗʰ 1738

Read again and Ordered that the further Consideration of this Petition be referred to the first tuesday of the next May Session and that James Minot and John Hobson Esq.ʳˢ with Such as the Honourable Board shall joine be a Committee at the Charge of the Petitioners to repair to the Lands petitioned for to be Erected into a Township first giving Seasonable notice as well to the petitioners as to the Inhabitants and Non Resident Proprietors of Lands within the s.ᵈ Towns of Dunstable and Groton of the time of their going by Causing the same to be publish'd in the Boston Gazette, that they carefully View the s.ᵈ Lands as well as the other parts of the s.ᵈ Towns, so farr as may be desired by the Partys or thought proper, that the Petitioners and all others Concerned be fully heard in their pleas and Allegations for, as well as against the prayer of the Petition ; and that upon Mature Consideration on the whole the Committee then report what in their Opinion may be proper for the Court to do in Answer there to   Sent up for Concurrence.

J Quincy Sp^{kr}

In Council Jan^{ry} 9th 1738

Read and Concurred and Thomas Berry Esqr is joined in the Affair

Simon Frost Dep^{ty} Sec^{ry}

Consented to   J. Belcher

A true Copy Exam^d per Simon Frost, Dep^y Sec^{ry}
In the House of Rep^{tives} June 7th 1739
Read and Concurred

J Quincy Sp^{kr}

[Massachusetts Archives, cxiv. 268-271.]

The Committee Appointed on the Petition of the Inhabitants and Proprietors situated on the Westerly side of Dunstable and Northerly side of Groton, Having after Notifying all parties, Repaired to the Lands, Petitioned to be Erected into a Township, Carefully Viewed the same, Find a very Good Tract of Land in Dunstable Westward of Nashaway River between s^d River and Souhegan River Extending from Groton New Grant and Townsend Line Six Miles East, lying in a very Commodious Form for a Township, and on said Lands there now is about Twenty Families, and many more settling, that none of the Inhabitants live nearer to a Meeting House then Seven miles and if they go to their own Town have to pass over a ferry the greatest part of the Year. We also Find in Groton a sufficient Quantity of Land accommodable for settlement, and a considerable Number of Inhabitants thereon, that in Some Short Time when they are well Agreed may be Erected into a Distinct Parish ; And that it will be very inconvenient to Erect a Township in the Form prayed for or to Break in upon Either Town. The Committee are of Opinion that the Petitioners in Dunstable are under such Circumstances as necessitates them to Ask Relief which will be fully Obtained by their being made Township, which if this Honble Court should Judge necessary to be done ; The Committee are Further of Opinion that it Will be greatly for the Good and Interest of the Township that the Non Resident Proprietors, have Liberty of Voting with the Inhabitants as to the Building and Placing a Meeting House and that the Lands be Equally Taxed, towards said House And that for the Support of the Gosple Ministry among them the Lands of the Non Resident Proprietors be Taxed at Two pence per Acre for the Space of Five Years.

All which is Humbly Submitted in the Name & by Order of the Committee

THOMAS BERRY

In Council July 7 1739

Read and ordered that the further Consideration of this Report be referred to the next Sitting, and that the Petitioners be in the meantime freed from paying anything toward the support of the ministry in the Towns to which they respectively belong

Sent down for Concurrence

J WILLARD Sec'y

In the House of Rep^tives June 7 : 1739
Read and Concurred

J QUINCY Sp^kr

Consented to   J BELCHER

In Council Decem^r 27, 1739.

Read again and Ordered that this Report be so far accepted as that the Lands mentioned and described therein, with the Inhabitants there be erected into a Separate & distinct precinct, and the Said Inhabitants are hereby vested with all Such Powers & Priviledges that any other Precinct in this Province have or by Law ought to enjoy and they are also impowered to assess & levy a Tax of Two pence per Acre per Annum for the Space of Five years on all the unimproved Lands belonging to the non resident Proprietors to be applied for the Support of the Ministry according to the Said Report.

Sent down for Concurrence

SIMON FROST Dep^y Sec^y

In the House of Rep^tives Dec 28. 1739
Read and Concur'd.

J QUINCY Sp^kr

Janu^a 1 : Consented to,   J BELCHER

[Massachusetts Archives, cxiv. 272, 273.]

While this petition was before the General Court, another one was presented praying for a new township to be made up from the same towns, but including a larger portion of Groton than was asked for in the first petition. This application met with bitter opposition on the part of both places, but it may have hastened the final action on the first petition. It resulted in setting off a precinct from Dunstable, under the name of the West Parish, which is now known as Hollis, New Hampshire. Some of the papers relating to the second petition are as follows: —

To His Excellency Jonathan Belcher Esquire Captain General and Governor in Chief in and over His Majesty's Province of the Massachusetts Bay in New England, the Honourable the Council and House of Representatives of said Province, in General Court Assembled Dec. 12th 1739.

The Petition of Richard Warner and Others, Inhabitants of the Towns of Groton and Dunstable.

Most Humbly Sheweth

That Your Petitioners dwell very far from the place of Public Worship in either of the said Towns, Many of them Eight Miles distant, some more, and none less than four miles, Whereby Your Petitioners are put to great difficulties in Travelling on the Lords Days, with our Families.

Your Petitioners therefore Humbly Pray Your Excellency and Honours to take their circumstances into your Wise and Compassionate Consideration, And that a part of the Town of Groton, Beginning at the line between Groton and Dunstable where it crosses Lancaster [Nashua] River, and so up the said River until it comes to a Place called and Known by the name of Joseph Blood's Ford Way on said River, thence a West Point 'till it comes to Townshend line &c. With such a part and so much of the Town of Dunstable as this Honourable Court in their great Wisdom shall think proper, with the Inhabitants Thereon, may be Erected into a separate and distinct Township, that so they may attend the Public Worship of God with more ease than at present they can, by reason of the great distance they live from the Places thereof as aforesaid.

And Your Petitioners, as in Duty bound, shall ever Pray &c.

Richard Warner Isaac Williams
Benjamin Swallow Ebenezer Gilson
William Allin Ebenezer Peirce
Samuel Fisk William Blood

John Green
Josiah Tucker
Zachariah Lawrence Junr

Jeremiah Lawrence
Stephen Eames

"[Inhabitants of Groton]"

Enoch Hunt
Eleazer Flegg
Samuel Cumings
William Blanchard
Gideon Howe

Josiah Blood
Samuel Parker
Samuel Farle
William Adams
Philip Wolrich

"[Inhabitants of Dunstable]"

In the House of Repr^{ves} Dec 12th 1739
Read and Sent up.

J Quincy Sp^{kr}

[Massachusetts Archives, cxiv. 274, 275.]

Province of the Massachusetts Bay
To His Excellency The Governour The Honble Council & House of Rep^{tives} in Generall Court Assembled Decr 1739

The Answer of ye Subscribers agents for the Town of Groton to ye Petition of Richard Warner & others praying that part of Said Town with part of Dunstable may be Erected into a Distinct & Seperate Township.

May it please your Excellency & Hon^{rs}

The Town of Groton Duely Assembled and Taking into Consideration ye Reasonableness of said Petition have Voted their Willingness, That the prayer of ye Petition be Granted as per their Vote herewith humbly presented appears, with this alteration namely That they Include the River (vizt Nashua River) over wch is a Bridge, built Intirely to accommodate said Petitioners heretofore, & your Respondents therefore apprehend it is but Just & Reasonable the same should for the future be by them maintain'd if they are Set of from us.

Your Respondents Pursuant to ye Vote Aforesaid, humbly move to your Excellency & Hon^{rs} That no more of Dunstable be Laid to Groton Then Groton have voted of, for one Great Reason that Induced Sundry of ye Inhabitants of Groton to come into Said Vote was This Namely They owning a very Considerable part of the Lands Voted to be set of as afores^d were willing to Condesent to ye Desires of their Neighbours apprehending that a meeting House being Erected on or near ye Groton Lands & a minister settled it would Raise their Lands in Vallue but should a considerable part of Dunstable be set of more then of Groton it must of course draw the Meeting House farther from y̓ᵉ Groton Inhabitants w̓ᶜʰ would be very hurtfull both to the people petitioners & those that will be Non Resident proprietors if the Township is made.

Wherefore they pray That Said New Township may be Incorporated Agreeable to Groton Vote viz̓ᵗ Made Equally out of both Towns & as in Duty bound Shall Ever pray

Nat^{ell} Sartell
William Lawrence

[Massachusetts Archives, cxiv. 278, 279.]

At A Legall town Meeting of the Inhabitants & free holders of the town of Groton assembled December y̓ᵉ 24ᵗʰ 1739 Voted & Chose Cap̓ᵗ William Lawrance Madderator for said meeting &c :

In Answer to the Petion of Richard Warnor & others Voted that the land with the Inhabitance mentioned in said Petion Including the Riuer from Dunstable Line to o̓ᶠ ford way Called and Known by y̓ᵉ Name of Joseph Bloods ford way: be Set of from the town of Groton to Joyn with sum of the westerdly Part of the town of Dunstable to make a Distinct and Sepprate town Ship Prouided that their be no : More taken from Dunstable then from Groton in making of Said new town. Also Voted that Nathaniel Sawtell Esq̓ʳ and Cap̓ᵗ William Lawrance be Agiants In the affair or Either of them to wait upon the Great and Generial Cort : to Vse their Best in Deauer to set off the Land as a fores̓ᵈ so that the one half of y̓ᵉ said New town may be made out of Groton and no : more.

Abstract Examined & Compaird of the town book of Record for Groton ⅌

Jona̓ᵗ Sheple Town Clark

Groton Decem̓ʰʳ 24ᵗʰ A : D : 1739

[Massachusetts Archives, cxiv. 281.]

Province of y̓ᵉ Mass̓ᵗˢ Bay

To His Excellency Jonathan Belcher Esq̓ʳ Governour &c To The Hon̓ᵈ His Majesty's Councill & House of Representatives in Gen̓ˡˡ Court Assembled December 1739

Whereas some few of the Inhabitants of Groton & Dunstable have Joyned in their Petition to this Hon̓ᵈ Court to be erected with Certain Lands into a Township as ⅌ their Petition entered the 12ᵗʰ Curr. which prayer if granted will very much Effect y̓ᵉ Quiet & Interest of the Inhabitants on the northerly part of Groton

Wherefore the Subscribers most Humbly begg leave To Remonstrate to y^or Excellency & Hon^rs the great & Numerous Damages that wee and many Others Shall Sustain if their Petition should be granted and would Humbly Shew

That the Contents of Groton is ab^t forty Thousand Acres Good Land Sufficient & happily Situated for Two Townships, and have on or near Two Hundred & Sixty Familys Setled there with Large Accomodations for many more

That the land pray'd for Out of Groton Could it be Spared is in a very Incomodious place, & will render a Division of the remaining part of the town Impracticable & no ways Shorten the travel of the remotest Inhabit^nts

That it will leave the town from the northeast and to the Southwest end at least fourteen miles and no possibillity for those ends to be Accomodated at any Other place wch will render the Difficulties we have long Laboured under without Remidy

That part of the lands Petitioned for (will when This Hon^d Court shall see meet to Divide us) be in & near the Middle of one of ye Townships

And Althô the number of thirteen persons is there Sett forth to Petition. it is wrong and Delusive Severall of them gave no Consent to any Such thing And to compleat their Guile have entered the names of four persons who has no Interest in that part of the town viz Swallow Tucker Ames & Green

That there is near Double the number On the Lands Petit^d for and Setled amongst them who Declare Against their Proceedings, & here Signifie the Same

That many of us now are at Least Seven miles from Our meeting And the Only Encouragement to Settle there was the undeniable Accomodations to make An Other town without wch We Should by no means have undertaken

That if this their Pet^n Should Succêd — Our hopes must Perish — thay by no means benifitted — & we put to all the Hardships Immaginable.

That the whole tract of Land thay pray may be Taken Out of groton Contains about Six or Seven Thousand Acres, (the Quantity and Situation may be Seen on ye plan herewith [ ]) And but Ab^t four Or five hundred Acres thereof Owned by the Peti^rs and but very Small Improvements On that. Under all wch Circumstances wee Humbly conceive it unreasonable for them to desire thus to Harrase and perplex us. Nor is it by Any means for the Accomodation of

Dunstable thus to Joyn who have land of their Own Sufficient and none to Spare without prejudicing their begun Settlement Wherefore we most Humbly pray Y:r Excellency & Hon:rs to compassionate Our Circumstances and that thay may not be set off and as in Duty bound &c

Benj:a Parker	John Shattuck
John Woods	Seth Phillips
Josiah Sartell	John Scott
Samuel Shattuck iu	Samuel Wright
Joseph Spoaldeng Juner	Benj:a Robines
James Larwance	John Swallow
Jonathan Shattuck	Isaac Woods
Nath:ll Parker	William Spoalding
James Shattuck	Enoch larwance
John Chambrlen	Jonathan Woods
Jacob Lakin	John Blood
John Cumings	Wiliam Cumings
Thomas Fisk	James Green
Henery Jefes	Nathaniel Lawrence iu
Isaac Lakin	Joseph Blood
David Shattuck	

[Massachusetts Archives, cxiv. 282-284.]

Wee the Sub:rs Inhab:ts of y:e Town of Dunstable & Resident in that part of it Called Nissitisitt Do hereby authorize and Fully Impower Abraham Taylor Jun:r and Peter Pawer to Represent to Gen:ll Court our unwillingness that any Part of Dunstable should [be] sett off to Groton to make a Township or Parish and to Shew forth our Earness Desire that a Township be maide intirely out out [sic] off Dunstable Land, Extending Six mils North from Groton Line which will Bring the[m] on the Line on y:e Brake of Land and Just Include the Present Setlers: or otherwise As y:e Hon:ll Commitee Reported and Agreeable to the tenour thereoff as The Hon:rd Court shall see meet and as in Duty bound &c

Tho:s Dinsmore,
(And 20 others.)

Dunstable Dece:r y:e 21:st 1739

These may sertifie to y:e Hon:rd Court that there is Nomber of Eleven more y:t has not signed this Nor y:e Petetion of Richard Worner & others, that is now setled and About to setle ·

[Massachusetts Archives, cxiv. 277.]

DUNSTABLE, HOLLIS, AND NOTTINGHAM. 63

At a very early period the Nashua River was sometimes called the Penacook and at other times the Groton River. In Thomas Noyes's survey of the grant of Major Simon Willard's farm in the autumn of 1659, the land is described as "lying and being for the most part on the east side of Groaten Riuer." And, again, at the session beginning on September 6, 1676, the approval of the General Court was given to Jonathan Danforth's survey of lands laid out to William Hauthorne, "lying in the wilderness; on the North of Groaten Riuer at a place called by the Indians Wistequassuck," now within the limits of Townsend. At a later period it was more frequently referred to as the Lancaster River; but the use of the present name, in the preceding papers, is the earliest instance that I have found among the Archives. Jonathan Danforth called it the Nashua River in his description of the survey of Groton, printed on page 14 of this book, and probably, also, in the first line of his description of Dunstable, printed on page 17, where the word is now almost wholly worn away. It is very likely that the river bore different names at different places along its course even at the same time.

II.

The running of the Provincial line in 1741 cut off a large part of Dunstable, and left it on the New Hampshire side of the boundary. It separated even the meeting-house and the burying-ground from that portion of the town still remaining in Massachusetts, and this fact added not a little to the deep animosity felt by the inhabitants when the disputed question was settled. It is no exaggeration to say that, throughout the old township, the feelings and sympathies of the inhabitants on both sides of the line were entirely with Massachusetts. A short time before this period the town of Nottingham had been incorporated by the General Court, and its territory taken from Dunstable. It comprised all the lands of that town lying on the easterly side of the Merrimack River; and the difficulty of attending public worship led to the division. When the Provincial line was established, it affected Nottingham, like many other towns, most unfavorably. It divided its territory, and left a tract of land in Massachusetts too small for a separate township, but by its associations and traditions belonging to Dunstable. This tract is to-day that part of Tyngsborough lying east of the river. The larger part of the town, by the new line, came under the jurisdiction of New Hampshire; but, as there was another town of Nottingham in the eastern quarter of that Province, the name was subsequently changed by an Act of Legislature, on July 5, 1746, to Nottingham West; and still later this was again changed on July 1, 1830, to Hudson.

The question of a new meeting-house was now agitating the inhabitants of Dunstable. Their former building was in another Province, where different laws prevailed respecting the qualifications and settlement of ministers. It was clearly evident that another structure must be built, and the customary dispute of small communities arose in regard to its site. Some persons favored one locality, and others another; some wanted the centre of territory, and others the centre of population. Akin to this subject I give the words of the Reverend Joseph Emerson, of Pepperell, — as quoted by Mr. Butler, in his History of Groton (page 306), — taken from a sermon delivered on March 8, 1770, at the dedication of the second meeting-house in Pepperell: "It hath been observed that some of the hottest contentions in this land hath been about settling of ministers and building meeting-houses; and what is the reason? The devil is a great enemy to settling ministers and building meeting-houses; wherefore he sets on his own children to work and make difficulties, and to the utmost of his power stirs up the corruptions of the children of God in some way to oppose or obstruct so good a work." This explanation was considered highly satisfactory, as the hand of the Evil One was always seen in such disputes.

During this period of local excitement an effort was made to annex Nottingham to Dunstable, and at the same time

Joint Grass to Dunstable. Joint Grass was a district in the northeastern part of Groton, settled by a few families, and named from a brook running through the neighborhood, which, in its turn, was so called from a peculiar kind of grass growing on its banks. It is evident from the documents that the questions of annexation and the site of the meeting-house were closely connected. The petition in favor of annexation was granted by the General Court on certain conditions, which were not fulfilled, and consequently the attempt fell to the ground. Some of the papers relating to it are as follows:

A Petition of sundry Inhabitants of the most northerly Part of the first Parish in *Groton*, praying that they may be set off from said *Groton* to *Dunstable*, for the Reasons mentioned.

Read and *Ordered*, That the Petitioners serve the Towns of *Groton* and *Dunstable* with Copies of this Petition, that they shew Cause, if any they have, on the first Friday of the next Sitting of this Court, why the Prayer thereof should not be granted.

Sent up for Concurrence.

[Journal of the House of Representatives (page 264), March 11, 1746.]

Francis Foxcroft, Esq; brought down the Petition of the northerly Part of *Groton*, as entred the 11th of *March* last, and refer'd. Pass'd in Council, *viz.* In Council *May* 29th 1747. Read again, together with the Answers of the Towns of *Groton* and *Dunstable*, and *Ordered*, That *Joseph Wilder* and *John Quincy*, Esqrs; together with such as the honourable House shall join, be a Committee to take under Consideration this Petition, together with the other Petitions and Papers referring to the Affair within mentioned, and report what they judge proper for this Court to do thereon.

Sent down for Concurrence.

Read and concur'd, and Major *Jones*, Mr. *Fox*, and Col. *Gerrish*, are joined in the Affair.

[Journal of the House of Representatives (page 11), May 29, 1747.]

John Hill, Esq; brought down the Petition of the Inhabitants of *Groton* and *Nottingham*, with the Report of a Committee of both Houses thereon.

Signed   JOSEPH WILDER, per Order.

Pass'd in Council, *viz.* In Council *June* 5th 1747. The within Report was read and accepted, and *Ordered*, That the Petition of *John Swallow* and others, Inhabitants of the northerly Part of *Groton* be so far granted, as that the Petitioners, with their Estates petition'd for, be set off from *Groton*, and annexed to the Town of *Dunstable*, agreable to *Groton* Town Vote of the 18th of *May* last; and that the Petition of the Inhabitants of *Nottingham* be granted, and that that Part of *Nottingham* left to the Province, with the Inhabitants thereon, be annexed to said *Dunstable*, and that they thus Incorporated, do Duty and receive Priviledges as other Towns within this Province do or by Law ought to enjoy.

And it is further *Ordered*, That the House for publick Worship be placed two Hundred and forty eight Rods distant from Mr. *John Tyng's* North-East Corner, to run from said Corner North fifty two Degrees West, or as near that Place as the Land will admit of.

Sent down for Concurrence.

Read and concur'd with the Amendment, *viz.* instead of those Words, . . . *And it is further* Ordered, *That the House for publick Worship be* . . . insert the following Words . . . *Provided that within one Year a House for the publick Worship of* GOD *be erected, and* . . .

Sent up for Concurrence.

[Journal of the House of Representatives (page 26), June 6, 1747.]

To his Excellency William Shirley Esquire Captain General and Governour in Chief in and over his Majestys Province of the Massachusetts Bay in New England The Honble the Council and Honble House of Representatives of the said Province in General Court Assembled at Boston the 31st of May 1749.

The petition of the Inhabitants of the Town of Dunstable in the Province of the Massachusetts Bay

Most Humbly Shew

That in the Year 1747, that part of Nottingham which lyes within this Government and part of the Town of Groton Called Joint Grass preferred two petitions to this Great and Honble Court praying that they might be Annexed to the Town of Dunstable which petitions Your Excellency and Honours were pleased to Grant upon Conditions that a meeting house for the Publick Worship of God should be built two hundred and forty Eight Rods 52 deg^s West of the

North from North East Corner of M.[r] John Tyngs land But the Inhabitants of the Town Apprehending Your Excellency and Honours were not fully Acquainted with the Inconveniencys that would Attend placeing the Meeting House there Soon after Convened in Publick Town Meeting Legally Called to Conclude upon a place for fixing said Meeting house where it would best Accommodate all the Inhabitants at which meeting proposals were made by some of the Inhabitants to take the Advice and Assistance of three men of other Towns which proposal was Accepted by the Town and they Accordingly made Choice of The Hon[ble] James Minot Esq.[r] Maj.[r] Lawrence and M.[r] Brewer and then Adjourned the Meeting.

That the said Gentlemen mett at the Towns Request and Determined upon a place for fixing the said Meeting house which was approved of by the Town and they Accordingly Voted to Raise the sum of one hundred pounds towards Defreying the Charge of Building the said House But Upon Reviewing the Spot pitched upon as aforesaid many of the Inhabitants Apprehended it was more to the southward than the Committee Intended it should be And thereupon a Meeting was Called on the Twenty Sixth day of May last when the Town voted to Build the meeting house on the East side of the Road that leads from Cap.[t] Cummings's to M[r] Simon Tompsons where some part of the Timber now lyes being about Forty Rods Northward of Isaac Colburns house which they Apprehended to be the Spot of Ground the Committee Intended to fix upon.

And for as much as the place Last Voted by the Town to Build their meeting house upon will best Accommodate all the Inhabitants,

Your pet.[rs] therefore most humbly pray Your Excellency and Honours would be pleased to Confirm the said Vote of the Town of the 26th day of May last and order the meeting house for the Publick Worship of God to be Erected on the peice of Ground aforementioned

And in duty bound they will ever pray &c

       Simon Tompson } Com[tee] for the
       Eben[r] Parkhurst } Town of Dunstable

[Massachusetts Archives, cxv. 507, 508.]

The Committee appointed on the Petition of a Committee for the Town of *Dunstable*, reported according to Order.

Read and accepted, and thereupon the following Order pass'd, viz. *In as much as the House for the publick Worship of* GOD *in* Dunstable *was not erected within the Line limitted in the Order of this Court of* June 6th 1747, *the Inhabitants of* Groton *and* Nottingham *have lost the Benefit of Incorporation with the Town of* Dunstable: Therefore

Voted, That a Meeting House for the publick Worship of GOD be erected as soon as may be on the East Side of the Road that leads from Capt. *Cummins* to *Simon Thompson's,* where the Timber for such a House now lies, agreable to a Vote of the said Town of *Dunstable* on the 26th of *May* last; and that the said Inhabitants of *Groton* and *Nottingham* be and continue to be set off and annexed to the Town of *Dunstable,* to do Duty and receive Priviledge there, their Neglect of Compliance with the said Order of *June* 6th 1747, notwithstanding, unless the major Part of the Inhabitants and rateable Estate belonging to said *Groton* and *Nottingham* respectively, shall on or before the first Day of *September* next in writing under their Hands, transmit to the Secretary's Office their Desire not to continue so incorporated with the town of *Dunstable* as aforesaid; provided also, That in Case the said Inhabitants of *Groton* and *Nottingham* shall signify such their Desire in Manner and Time as aforesaid, they be nevertheless subjected to pay and dischàrge their Proportion of all Publick Town or Ministerial Rates or Taxes hitherto granted or regularly laid on them; excepting the last Sum granted for building a Meeting House. And that the present Town Officers stand and execute their Offices respectively until the Anniversary Town-Meeting at *Dunstable* in *March* next.

Sent up for Concurrence.

[Journal of the House of Representatives (pages 46, 47), June 26, 1749.]

Whereas the Great & Generall Court of the the [*sic*] Province of the Massachusetts Bay in June Last, On the Petitions of Dunstable & Nottingham has Ordered that the Inhabitants of Groton and Nottingham, Which by Order of the s^d Court the 6th of June 1747 Were On Certain Conditions Annexed to s^d Dunstable & (Which Conditions not being Complyed with) be Annexed to s^d Dunstable to do duty & Receive priviledge there their neglect of Complyance notwithstanding, Unless the major part of the Inhabitants and ratable Estate belonging to the s^d Groton & Nottingham respectively Shall on or before the first day of September next in Writing under their hands Transmitt to the Secretarys Office their desire not to Continue so Incorporated With the town of Dunstable as afores^d Now therefore Wee the Subscribers Inhabitants of Groton & Nottingham Sett of as afores^d do hereby Signifie Our desire not to Continue so Incorporated with the town of Dunstable as afores^d but to be Sett at Liberty As tho that Order of Court had not ben passed

Dated the 10th day of July 1749

Inhabitants of Groton

Timothy Read
Joseph fletcher
John Swallow

Samuel Comings
Benjamin Robbins
Joseph Spalding iuner

Inhabitants of Nottingham

Samuell Gould
Robert Fletcher
Joseph perriaham Daken [Deacon?]

iohn Collans
Zacheus Spaulding
(And ten others.)

[Massachusetts Archives, cxv. 515.]

A manuscript plan of Dunstable, made by Joseph Blanchard in the autumn of 1748, and accompanying these papers among the Archives (cxv. 516), is of considerable interest to the local antiquary.

In the course of a few years most of the Groton signers reconsidered the matter, and changed their minds. It appears from the following communication that the question of the site of the meeting-house had some influence in the matter : —

Groton, May 10, 1753. We have concluded to Joine with Dunstable in settling the gospell and all other affairs hart & hand in case Dunstable woud meet us in erecting a meting house in center of Lands or center of Travel.

JOSEPH SPAULDING Jr.
JOHN SWALLOW.
TIMOTHY READ.
SAMUEL CUMINGS.
JOSEPH PARKHURST.

[Nason's History of Dunstable, page 85.]

The desired result of annexation was now brought about, and in this way Joint Grass became a part and parcel of Dunstable. The following extracts give further particulars in regard to it: —

A Petition of a Committee in Behalf of the Inhabitants of *Dunstable*, within this Province, shewing, that that Part of *Dunstable* by the late running of the Line is small, and the Land much broken, unable to support the Ministry, and other necessary Charges; that there is a small Part of *Groton* contiguous, and well situated to be united to them in the same Incorporation, lying to the West and Northwest of them; that in the Year 1744, the Inhabitants there requested them that they might be incorporated with them, which was conceeded to by the Town of *Groton;* that in Consequence of this, upon Application to this Court, they were annexed to the Town of *Dunstable* with the following Proviso, *viz*. "That within one Year from that Time a House for the publick Worship of GOD should be erected at a certain Place therein mentioned:" Which Place was esteemed by all Parties both in *Groton* & *Nottingham*, so incommodious, that it was not complied withal; that on a further Application to this Court to alter the Place, Liberty was given to the Inhabitants of *Groton* and *Nottingham*, to withdraw, whereby they are deprived of that contiguous and necessary Assistance which they expected: Now as the Reasons hold good in every Respect for their Incorporation with them, they humbly pray that the said Inhabitants of *Groton* by the same Bounds as in the former Order stated, may be reannexed to them, for the Reasons mentioned.

Read and *Ordered*, That the Petitioners serve the Inhabitants of *Groton* therein refer'd to, as also the Clerk of the Town of *Groton*, with Copies of this Petition, that so the said Inhabitants, as also the Town of *Groton*, shew Cause, if any they have, on the first Tuesday of the next *May* Session, why the Prayer thereof should not be granted.

Sent up for Concurrence.

[Journal of the House of Representatives (pages 138, 139), April 4, 1753.]

John Hill, Esq; brought down the Petition of a Committee of the Town of *Dunstable*, as entred the 4th of *April* last, and refer'd. Pass'd in Council, *viz*, In Council *June* 5th 1753. Read again, together with the Answer of the Inhabitants of that Part of *Groton* commonly called *Joint-Grass*, and likewise *William Lawrence*, Esq ; being heard in Behalf of the Town of *Groton*, and the Matter being fully considered, *Ordered*, That the Prayer of the Petition be so far granted, as that *Joseph Fletcher*, *Joseph Spaulding*, *Samuel Comings*, *Benjamin Robbins*, *Timothy Read*, *John Swallow*, *Joseph Parkhurst*, and *Ebenezer Parkhurst*, Jun. with their Families and Estates, and other Lands petitioned for, be set off from the Town of *Groton*, and annexed to the town of *Dunstable*, agreable to the Vote of the Town of *Groton* on the 18th of *May* 1747, to receive Priviledge and do Duty there, provided that *Timothy Read*, Constable for the Town of *Groton*, and Collector of the said Parish in said Town the last Year, and *Joseph Fletcher*, Constable for the said Town this present Year, finish their Collection of the Taxes committed or to be committed to them respectively ; and also that the said Inhabitants pay their Proportion of the Taxes that are already due or shall be due to the said Town of *Groton* for the present Year, for which they may be taxed by the Assessors of *Groton*, as tho' this Order had not past : provided also that the Meeting-House for the publick Worship of GOD in *Dunstable* be erected agreable to the Vote of *Dunstable* relating thereto in *May* 1753. Sent down for Concurrence.

Read and concur'd.

[Journal of the House of Representatives (page 21), June 7, 1753.]

The part of Nottingham mentioned in these petitions was not joined to Dunstable until the next year. On June 14, 1754, an order passed the House of Representatives, annexing "a very small Part of Nottingham now lying in this Province, unable to be made into a District, but very commodious for Dunstable," — according to the printed Journal ; and on the same day it received the assent of the Governor and Council.

VI.

PEPPERELL.

THE west parish of Groton was set off as a precinct on November 26, 1742. It comprised that part of the town lying on the west side of the Nashua River, north of the road from Groton to Townsend. Its incorporation as a parish or precinct allowed the inhabitants to manage their own ecclesiastical affairs, while in all other matters they continued to act with the parent town. Its partial separation gave them the benefit of a settled minister in their neighborhood, which in those days was considered of great importance.

It is an interesting fact to note that in early times the main reason given in the petitions for dividing towns was the long distance to the meeting-house, by which the inhabitants were prevented from hearing the stated preaching of the gospel.

The petitioners for the change first asked for a township, which was not granted; but subsequently they changed their request to a precinct instead, which was duly allowed. The papers relating to the matter are as follows: —

Province of The Massechuetts Bay in New England.

To His Excellency Wm Shirley, Esqr Goveiner in & over ye Same And To The Hon^{le} his Majestis Council & House of Repre- sentetives in Gen^{ll} Court Assembled June 1742:

The Petition of Sundry Inhabitants & Resendant in the North- erly Part of Groton Humbly Sheweth that the Town of Groton is at Least ten miles in Length North & South & seven miles in wedth East & West And that in Runing two miles Due North from the Present Meeting House & from thence to Run Due East to Dunstable West Line. And from the Ende of the S^d two miles to Run West till it Comes to the Cuntry Rode that is Laide out to Townshend & so on S^d Rode till it Comes to Townshend East Line then tur[n]ing & Runing Northly to Nestiquaset Corner which is for Groton & Townshend then tur[n]ing & Runing Easterly on Dunstable South Line & So on Dunstable Line till it comes to the Line first mentioned, Which Land Lyeth about Seven miles in Length & four miles & a Quarter in Wedth.

And Thare is Now Setled in those Lines here after mentioned is about the Number of Seventy families all Redy And may [many?] more ready to Settle there and as soon as scet off to the Petitioners & those families Settled in ye Lines afore s^d Would make A Good township & the Remaining Part of Groton Left in a regular forme And by reason of the great Distance your Petitioners are from the Present Meeting House are put to very Great Disadvantages in Attending the Public Worship of God many of Whom are Oblidged to travel Seven or Eight miles & that the Remaining Part of Groton Consisting of such good land & ye Inhabitants so Numerous that thay Can by no means be Hurt Should your Petitioners & those families Settled in ye Lines afore s^d Be Erected to a Seprate & Distinct Township ; That the in Contestable situation & accomodation on the s^d Lands was ye one great reason of your Petitioners Setling thare & Had Not those Prospects been so Clear to us We should by no means have under taken The Hardship We have already & must go Throu.

Wherefore Your Petitioners Would farther Shew that Part of ye Land here Prayed for all Redy Voted of by the S^d town to be a Presinct & that the most of them that are in that Lines have Subscribed with us to be a Dest[i]ncte Township Wherefore Your Petitioners Humbly Pray your Honnors to Grante us our Desire according to This our Request as we in Duty Bound Shall Ever Pray &c

  Joseph Spaulding iur   William Blood
  Zachariah Lawrance   Nathaniel Parker
  William Allen   Enoch Lawarnce
  Jeremiah Lawrance   Samuel Right

James larwance	Isacc laken
Josiah Tucker	Isacc Williams
Sam^{ll} fisk	John Swallow
Solomon blood	Joseph Swallow
John Woods	Benjn Robins
Josiah Sartell	Nathan Fisk
benj^{n} Swallow	John Chamberlin
Elies Ellat	Jacob Lakin
Richard Worner	Seth Phillips
Ebenezer Gillson	John Cumings
Ebenezer Parce	Benjn Parker
James Blood iu	Gersham Hobart
Joseph Spaulding	Joseph Lawrance
Phiniahas Parker jur	John Spaulding
Joseph Warner	Isaac Woods
Phineahas Chambrlin	

In the House of Rep^{ives} June. 10. 1742

Read and Ordered that the Pet^{rs} serve the Town of Groton with a Copy of this Pet^{n} that they shew cause if any they have on the first fryday of the next session of this Court why the Prayer thereof should not be granted

Sent up for concurrence
T Cushing Spkr

In Council June 15. 1742 ;
Read & Non Concur'd

J Willard Secry

[Massachusetts Archives, cxiv. 779, 780.]

To his Excellency William Shirley Esqr Captain General and Governour in Cheiff in and over his Majesties Province of ye Massachusetts Bay in New England : To ye Honourable his Majesties Council and House of Representatives in General Court Assembled on ye Twenty sixth Day of May. A: D. 1742.

The Petition of us the Subscribers to your Excellency and Honours Humbley Sheweth that we are Proprietors and Inhabitants of ye Land Lying on ye Westerly Side Lancester River (so called) [now known as the Nashua River] in ye North west corner of ye Township of Groton : & Such of us as are Inhabitants thereon Live very Remote from ye Publick worship of God in s^{d} Town and at many Times and Season of y.ͤ year are Put to Great Difficulty to attend y.ͤ same: And the Lands Bounded as Followeth (viz) Southerly on Townshend Rode: Westerly on Townshend Line: Northerly on Dunstable West Precinct, & old Town: and Easterly on said River as it now Runs to y.ͤ First mentioned Bounds. being of y.ͤ Contents of about Four Miles Square of Good Land, well Scituated for a Precint: And the Town of Groton hath been Petitioned to Set of y.ͤ Lands bounded as afores.ᵈ to be a Distinct and Seperate Precint and at a Town Meeting of y.ͤ Inhabitants of s.ᵈ Town of Groton Assembled on y.ͤ Twenty Fifth Day of May Last Past The Town voted y.ͤ Prayer of y.ͤ s.ᵈ Petition and that y.ͤ Lands before Described should be a Separate Precinct and that y.ͤ Inhabitants thereon and Such others as hereafter Shall Settle on s.ᵈ Lands should have y.ͤ Powers and Priviledges that other Precincts in s.ᵈ Province have or Do Enjoy: as p.ͬ a Coppy from Groton Town Book herewith Exhibited may Appear &c: For the Reasons mentioned we the Subscribers as afores.ᵈ Humbley Prayes your Excellency and Honours to Set off y.ͤ s.ᵈ Lands bounded as afores.ᵈ to be a Distinct and Sepperate Precinct and Invest y.ͤ Inhabitants thereon (Containing about y.ͤ N.ͦ of Forty Famelies) and Such others as Shall hereafter Settle on s.ᵈ Lands with Such Powers & Priviledges as other Precincts in s.ᵈ Province have &c or Grant to your Petitioners Such other Releaf in y.ͤ Premises as your Excellency and Honours in your Great Wisdom Shall think Fit: and your Petitioners as in Duty bound Shall Ever pray &c.

Benj Swallow	Moses Woods
W.ᵐ Spalden	Zachery Lawrence Jun.ʳ
Isaac Williams	Jeremiah Lawrence
Ebenezer Gilson	John Mozier
Elias Ellit	Josiah Tucker
Samuel Shattuck iu	W.ᵐ Allen
James Shattuck	John Shadd
David Shattuck	Jam.ˢ Green
David Blood .	John Kemp
Jonathan Woods	Nehemiah Jewett
John Blood iuner	Eleazar Green
Josiah Parker	Jonathan Shattuck
Jacob Ames	Jonathan Shattuck Jun.ʳ
Jonas Varnum	

In the House of Rep^{tives} Novr. 26. 1742

In Answer to the within Petition ordered that that Part of the Town of Groton Lying on the Westerly Side of Lancaster River within the following bounds vizt bounding Easterly on said River Southerly on Townsend Road so called Westerly on Townsend line and Northerly on Dunstable West Precinct with the Inhabitants thereon be and hereby are set off a distinct and seperate precinct and Vested with the powers & previledges which other Precincts do or by Law ought to enjoy always provided that the Inhabitants Dwelling on the Lands abovementioned be subject to pay their Just part and proportions of all ministeriall Rates and Taxes in the Town of Groton already Granted or Assessed

Sent up for Concurrence

             T Cushing Spk^r

In Council Novr. 26 1742 Read and Concurr'd

             J Willard Secry

       Consented to,   W Shirley.

[Massachusetts Archives, cxiv. 768, 769.]

When the Provincial line was run between Massachusetts and New Hampshire, in the spring of 1741, it left a gore of land, previously belonging to the west parish of Dunstable, lying north of the territory of Groton and contiguous to it. It formed a narrow strip, perhaps three hundred rods in width at the western end, running easterly for nearly four miles and tapering off to a point a short distance west of the Nashua River, by which stream it was entirely separated from Dunstable. Shaped like a thin wedge, it lay along the border of the Province, and belonged geographically to the west precinct or parish of Groton. Under these circumstances the west or second parish petitioned the General Court to have it annexed to their jurisdiction, which request was granted. William Prescott, one of the committee appointed to take charge of the matter, nearly a quarter of a century later was the commander of the American forces at the Battle of Bunker Hill. It has been incorrectly stated by writers that this triangular parcel of land was the gore ceded, in the summer of 1736, to the proprietors of Groton, on the petition of Benjamin Prescott. The documents relating to this matter are as follows : —

To his Honnor Spencer Phipes Esqr Capt Geniorl and Commander In Cheaf in and ouer his majists prouince of the Massachusets Bay in New england and to The Honble his majestys Councel and House of Representatiues In Geniral Courte assambled at Boston The 26 of December 1751

The Petition of Peleg Lawrance Jarimah Lawrance and william Prescott a Cum^{ttee} for the Second Parish In Groton in The County of Middle sikes

Humbly Shew That Theare is a strip of Land of about fiue or six hundred acors Lys ajoyning To The Town of Groton which be Longs To the town of Dunstable the said strip of land Lys near fouer mill in Length and bounds on the North Line of the said second Parrish in Groton and on the South Side of Newhampsher Line which Peeace by Runing the sd Line of Newhampsher was Intierly Cut off from the town of Dunstable from Receueing any Priuelidge their for it Lys not Less then aboute Eight mill from the Senter of the town of Dunstable and but about two mill and a half from the meeting house in the said second Parish in Groton so that they that settel on the sd Strip of Land may be much beter acommadated to be Joyned to ye town of Groton and to the sd second Parish than Euer thay Can any other way in this Prouince and the town of Dunstable being well sencable thare of haue at thare town meeting on the 19 Day of December Currant voted of the sd Strip of Land allso James Colburn who now Liues on sd Strip Land from the town of Dunstable to be annexed to the town of Groton and to the sd second Parish in sd town and the second Parish haue aCordingly voted to Recue the same all which may appear by the vote of sd Dunstable and said Parish which will be of Grate advantige to the owners of the sd strip of Land and a benefit to the said second Parish in Groton so that your Petitioners Humbly Pray that the sd strip of Land may be annexed to the said second Parish in Groton so far as Groton Nor west corner to do Duty and Recue Priulidge theare and your petionrs In Duty bound shall Euer Pray

Peleg Lawrence
Will^M Prescott
Jeremiah Lawrence

Dunstable December 24 1751

this may Certifye the Grate and Genirol Courte that I Liue on the slip of Land within mentioned and it tis my Desier that the prayer of this Petition be Granted

JAMES COLBURN

In the House of Rep[tives] Jan[ry] 4. 1752

Voted that the prayer of the Petition be so farr granted that the said strip of Land prayed for, that is the Jurisdiction of it be Annex'd to the Town of Groton & to y[e] Second Precinct in said Town & to doe dutys there & to recieve Priviledges from them.

Sent up for Concurrence

T. HUBBARD Spk[r]

In Council Jan[y] 6. 1752   Read & Concur'd

J WILLARD Secry.

Consented to,   S PHIPS

[Massachusetts Archives, cxvi. 162, 163.]

At this period the Crown authorities were jealous of the growth of the popular party in the House of Representatives, and for that reason they frowned on every attempt to increase the number of its members. This fact had some connection with the tendency, which began to crop out during Governor Shirley's administration, to form districts instead of towns, thereby withholding their representation.

The west parish of Groton was made a district on April 12, 1753, the day the Act was signed by the Governor, which was a second step toward its final and complete separation. It then took the name of Pepperrell, and was vested with still broader political powers. It was so called after Sir William Pepperrell, who had successfully commanded the New England troops against Louisburg; and the name was suggested, doubtless, by the Reverend Joseph Emerson, the first settled minister of the parish. He had accompanied that famous expedition in the capacity of chaplain, only the year before he had received a call for his settlement, and his associations with the commander were fresh in his memory. It will be noticed that the Act for incorporating the district leaves the name blank, which was customary in this kind of legislation at that period; and the Governor, perhaps with the advice of his Council, was in the habit subsequently of filling out the name.

Pepperell — for one "r" has been dropped from the name[1] — had now all the privileges of a town, except the right to choose a representative to the General Court, and this political connection with Groton was kept up until the beginning of the Revolution. In the session of the General Court which met at Watertown on July 19, 1775, Pepperell was represented by a member, and in this way acquired the privileges of a town without any special act of incorporation. Other similar districts were likewise represented, in accordance with the precept calling that body together, and thus they obtained municipal rights without the usual formality. The precedent seems to have been set by the First Provincial Congress of Massachusetts, which met in the autumn of 1774, and was made up of delegates from the districts as well as from the towns. It was a revolutionary step taken outside of the law. On March 23, 1786, this anomalous condition of affairs was settled by an Act of the Legislature, which declared all districts incorporated before January 1, 1777, to be towns for all intents and purposes.

The Act for the incorporation of the district of Pepperell is as follows: —

Anno Regni Regis Georgij Secundi vicesimo Sexto

An Act for Erecting the second Precinct in the Town of Groton into a seperate District

Be it enacted by the Leiu:t Gov:r Council and House of Representatives

That the second Precinct in Groton bounding Southerly on the old Country Road leading to Townshend, Westerly on Townshend Line Northerly on the Line last run by the Governm:t of New Hampshire as the Boundary betwixt that Province and this Easterly to the

---

[1] It was near the end of the last century that the practice began of writing the name of the town with one "r," though it was many years before the custom became general.

middle of the River, called Lancaster [Nashua] River, from where the said Boundary Line crosses said River, so up the middle of y.ᵉ said River to where the Bridge did stand, called Kemps Bridge, to the Road first mentioned, be & hereby is erected into a seperate District by the Name of   and that the said District be and hereby is invested with all the Priviledges Powers and Immunities that Towns in this Province by Law do or may enjoy, that of sending a Representative to the generall Assembly only excepted, and that the Inhabitants of said District shall have full power & Right from Time to time to joyn with the s.ᵈ Town of Groton in the choice of Representative or Representatives, in which Choice they shall enjoy all the Priviledges which by Law they would have been entitled to, if this Act had not been made. And that the said District shall from Time to time pay their proportionable part of the Expence of such Representative or Representatives According to their respective proportions of y.ᵉ Province Tax.

And that the s.ᵈ Town of Groton as often as they shall call a Meeting for the Choice of a Representative shall give seasonable Notice to the Clerk of said District for the Time being, of the Time and place of holding such Meeting, to the End that aid Districts may join them therein, and the Clerk of said District shall set up in some publick place in s.ᵈ District a Notification thereof accordingly or otherwise give Seasonable Notice, as the District shall determine.

Provided Nevertheless and be it further enacted That the said District shall pay their proportion : of all Town County and Province Taxes already set on or granted to be raised by s.ᵈ Town as if this Act had not been made, and also be at one half the charge in building and repairing the Two Bridges on Lancaster River aforesaid in s.ᵈ District.

Provided also and be it further Enacted That no poor Persons residing in said District and Who have been Warn'd by the Selectmen of said Groton to depart s.ᵈ Town shall be understood as hereby exempted from any Process they would have been exposed to if this Act had not been made.

And be it further enacted that W.ᵐ Lawrence[1] Esq.ʳ Be and hereby is impowered to issue his Warrant directed to some principal Inhabitant in s.ᵈ District requiring him to notify the Inhabitants of said District to meet at such Time & place as he shall appoint to

---

[1] This name apparently inserted after the original draft was made.

choose all such Officers as by Law they are Impowered to Choose for conducting the Affairs of s^d District.

In the House of Rep^{lives} April 5, 1753
Read three several times and pass'd to be Engross'd
Sent up for Concurrence

T. HUBBARD Spk^r

In Council April 5 1753 AM
Read a first and Second Time and pass'd a Concurrence

THO^s CLARKE Dp^{ty} Sec̃ry

[Massachusetts Archives, cxvi. 360-362.]

VII.

SHIRLEY, TYNGSBOROUGH, AND AYER.

About this time it was proposed to form a new township from Groton, Lancaster, and Harvard, including a small parcel of land known as Stow Leg, a strip of territory perhaps two hundred rods in width and two miles in length, lying west of the Nashua River. This "Leg" had belonged originally to Stow, but had become wholly detached from that town by the incorporation of Harvard. The proposed township covered nearly the same territory as that now occupied by Shirley. The attempt, however, does not appear to have been successful. The following covenant, signed by certain inhabitants of the towns interested in the movement, is on file, and with it a rough plan of the neighborhood; but I find no other allusion to the matter either in petitions or records : —

We the Subscribers being Inhabitants of the Extream Parts of Groton Lancaster and Harvard as allso the Proprietors of the Land belonging to the Town of Stow (which Land is Scituate Lying and being Betwen the Towns above said Namely Groton Lancaster and Harvard) Do Covenant and Promise to and with Each other And We Do Hereby of our own Free Will and Motion In the Exercise of Love and Charity Towards one another with Mutual Consent in the strongest Manner Binding our Selves the Subscribers each and every of us Conjointly one to another (for the Gosples Sake) Firmly Covenantng and Promising to and with Each other that we will as Speedely as may be with Conveniency Petition the Several Towns to which we Respectively belong and Likewise the Great and General Court That we may be Erected or Incorporated into a Destinct and seperate Township of our Selves with those Lands within the Bounds and Limits Here after Discribed viz Beginning at the River called Lancaster [Nashua] River at the turning of Sd River Below the Brige called John Whits Brige & Runing Northerly to Hell Pond and on Still to the Line Betwixt Harvard and Groton Including John Farwell then to Coyecus Brook Leaveing the Mills and Down Said Brook to the River and down Said River to the Rye ford way then Runing Westerly to the Northerly End of Horse Pond & so on to Luningburg Line Including Robert Henry & Daniel Page and then Runing Southerly Extendig Beyound Luningburg So far Into Lancaster as that Running Easterly the Place on which Relph Kindal formerly Lived Shall be Included and so on Running Easterly to the Turn in the River first mentioned

Moreover we Do Covenant Promise and Engage Truly and Faithfuly that we will Consent to and Justifie any Petition that Shall be Prefered in our names and behalf to our Respective Towns and to the Great & General Court for the Ends and Purposes above Mentioned

Furthermore we Do Covenant Promise and Engage as above that we will advance money for and Pay all Such Reasonable and necessary Charges that may arise in the Prosecuting and Obtaining our Said Petitions and that we will Each and Every of us Respectively Endever to Promote and Maintain Peace Unity Concord and Good Agreement amoungst our Selves as Becometh Christians

And now haveing thus Covenanted as above Said We Do Each and Every one of us who have Hereunto Subscribed Protest and Declare that Every Article and Parigraph and Thing Containd in the above Writen Shall be Absolutely and Unacceptionably Binding in Manner and form as above Declared and Shall So Continue upon and Against Each and Every one of us untill we are Erected or Incorporated Into a Township as above said or that Provedance Shall Remove us by Death or Otherways any thing to the Conterary Notwithstanding

Witness our Hands the Eighth Day of December one Thousand Seven Hundred and Fourty Seven and in the Twentieth Year Of His Majesties Reign Georg the Secund King &c

Harvard

Richard hall	Amos Russll
Jonⁿ Bigelow	Johnathan —^{His} Read _{mark}
Joseph Hutchins	
Simeon Farnworth	Jonathan Read iu
Timothy hall	Abijah Willard
Phenihas Farnsworth	

Groton

Samuel Hazen	John Longley jn^r
Joseph Preist	Abijah Willard
Samll flood	Manasser Divoll
John pearce	John Osgood
Charles Richards	Abijah Frost
Daniel Page	John Peirce hous rite

Lancaster

Henry Haskell	William Farmer
John Nicholls	Joseph Bond
Thomas Wright	Henry Willard
William Willard	Benjamin Willard
Joshua Johnson	Jacob Houghton
Daniel Willard	Corp Elias Sawyer
Joseph Priest	Amos Am^{his} Atherton _{mark}

Stow

John Houghton Ju	Hannah Brown
John Sampson	Samuel Randal
Joseph Brown	Benjamin Samson

[Massachusetts Archives, cxv. 220–222.]

Hell Pond, mentioned in this covenant, is situated in the northwest part of Harvard, and so called "from its amazing depth," says the Reverend Peter Whitney, in the History of Worcester County (page 158).

The following petition refers to an unsuccessful attempt made during this period to form a second precinct within the township. The petitioners lived in that part of Groton which afterward became the district of Shirley : —

To the Inhabitants of the Town of Groton assembled in Town meeting on the first Day of March 1747

The petition of us the Subscribers being all Inhabitants of the Town of Groton a fore sd humbly Shueth that your petitioners all Live in the Extreem parts of the Town and by that means we are Incapacatated to attend the publick worship constantly Either our selves or famelies and and [sic] being Sensable that our being set off in order for a presinct will be of Great Seruis to us we Desire that we may be set of by the bounds following Viz begining at the mouth of Squa[n]ikook Riuer and so Run vp sd Riuer till it Comes to Townshend Line and then by Townshend and Lunenburgh Lines till it Cometh to Groton South west Cornor and so by the South Line of Said Town vntill It Cometh to Lancaster [Nashua] Riuer and then Down sd Riuer till it cometh to haruard Cornor and Then about a mile on haruard North Line then Turn North and Run to the wast brook in Coicors [Nonacoicus] farm whear peeple Generally pass ouer and from thence to The mouth of Squanikook Riuer whear we first began and your petetioners as bound in Duty Shall Ever pray &c

January th 26 1747

John Whitney	William Simonds
John Williams	William Preston
Dauid Gould	William Williams
John Kelcey	henery farwell
Phinehas burt	Josiah farwell
Joseph Wilson	John z Russell his / mark
Tho⁵ Laughton	
James Pattorson	James Park
Jonathan Gould	Jacob x Williams his / mark
Robert henry	
John Williams Jr	Danell x Page his / mark
William farneth	
Jonas Longley	Joseph x Dodge his / mark
Almer farwell	moses bennett Jun
Isaac holdin	Caleb bartlit
Jerathmel power	Francis harris
Philemon holdin	Caleb holdin
Stephen holdin Ju	hezekiah Sawtell Jr

The aboue petetion being Red at the annauarsory meeting in Groton on march th 1 1747 and the prayer thear of Granted Except the Land on the Easterly Side Lancaster Riuer

       and Recorded ℞
           Thos Tarbell
            Town Clerk

[Town Records, iv. 57.]

A year or two later another attempt was made to divide the town, but it did not succeed. The lines of the proposed township included nearly the same territory as the present ones of Shirley. The following references to the scheme are found, under their respective dates, in the Journal of the House of Representatives: —

A Petition of sundry Inhabitants of *Groton* and *Lunenburg*, praying they may be erected into a distinct and seperate Township or Precinct, agreable to the Plan therewith exhibited, for the Reasons mentioned.

Read and *Ordered*, That the Petitioners serve the Town of *Lunenburg*, and the first Parish in *Groton*, with Copies of this Petition, that they shew Cause, if any they have, on the 29th of *December* next, if the Court be then Sitting, if not on the first Friday of the next Sitting of this Court, why the Prayer thereof should not be granted.

          Sent up for Concurrence.

[Journal of the House of Representatives (page 100), November 30, 1749.]

Samuel Watts, Esq; brought down the Petition of sundry Inhabitants of *Lunenburg* and *Groton*, as entred the 30th of *November* last, and refer'd. Pass'd in Council, *viz*. In Council *December* 29th 1749. Read again, with the Answer of the Town of *Lunenburg*, and *Ordered*, That the Consideration of this Petition be refer'd to the second Wednesday of the next Sitting of this Court. Sent down for Concurrence.

With a Petition from sundry Inhabitants of *Lunenburg*, praying to be set off from said Town of *Leominster*. Pass'd in Council, *viz* In Council *December* 29th 1749. Read and *Ordered*, That the Petitioners serve the Town of *Lunenburg*, with a Copy of this Petition, that they shew Cause, if any they have, on the second Wednesday

of the next Sitting of this Court, why the Prayer thereof should not be granted.
Sent up for Concurrence.

[Journal of the House of Representatives (page 142), December 29, 1749.]

John Chandler, Esq; brought down the Petitions of *John Whitney,* and others of the westerly Part of *Groton,* and the easterly Part of the Town of *Lunenburgh,* and *Edward Hartwell,* Esq; and others of said Town, Pass'd in Council, *viz.* In Council *April* 4th 1750. Ordered, That *Samuel Watts, James Minot,* and *John Otis,* Esqrs; with such as the honourable House shall join, be a Committee to consider the Petitions above-mentioned, and the several Answers thereto, hear the Parties, and report what they judge proper for the Court to do thereon.
Sent down for Concurrence.

Read and concur'd, and Mr. *Rice,* Capt. *Livermore,* Col. *Richards,* and Mr. *Daniel Pierce,* are joined in the Affair.

[Journal of the House of Representatives (page 214), April 5, 1750.]

Joseph Wilder, Esq., brought down the Report of a Committee of both Houses, on the Petition of *John Whitney,* and others, as entred the 30th. of *November* last, and refer'd. Signed *James Minott,* per Order.

Pass'd in Council, *viz.* In Council *June* 21, 1750. Read and *Voted,* That this Report be not accepted, and that the Petition of *John Whitney* and others therein refer'd to, be accordingly dismiss'd, and that the Petitioners pay the Charge of the Committee.

Sent down for Concurrence. Read and concur'd.

[Journal of the House of Representatives (page 41), June 22, 1750.]

A Petition of sundry Inhabitants of the westerly Part of *Groton,* and the easterly Part of *Lunenburg,* praying that their Memorial and Report thereon, which was dismiss'd the 22d of *June* last, may be revived and reconsidered, for the Reasons mentioned.

Read and *Ordered,* That Mr. *Turner,* Mr. *Tyng,* and Major *Jones* with such as the honourable Board shall join, be a Committee to take this Petition under Consideration, and report what they judge proper to be done thereon. Sent up for Concurrence.

[Journal of the House of Representatives (pages 76, 77), October 3, 1750.]

John Greenleafe, Esq. ; brought down the Petition of sundry Inhabitants of *Groton* and *Lunenburg*, as entred the 3d Currant, and referr'd. Pass'd in Council, *viz.* In Council *October* 3d 1750. Read and nonconcur'd, and *Ordered*, That this Petition be dismiss'd.
Sent down for Concurrence.

Read and nonconcur'd, and *Ordered*, That the Petitioner serve the Town of *Lunenburg* with a Copy of this Petition, that they shew Cause, if any they have, on the second Wednesday of the next Sitting of this Court, why the Prayer thereof should not be granted.
Sent up for Concurrence.

[Journal of the House of Representatives (page 93), October 9, 1750.]

A Memorial of *John Whitney* and others of the Southwesterly Part of *Groton*, praying that their Petition exhibited in *November* 1749, may be revived, and the Papers prefer'd at that Time again considered, for the Reasons mentioned.

Read and *Ordered*, That the Petition lie on the Table.

[Journal of the House of Representatives (page 64), October 9, 1751.]

Ordered, That the Petition of *John Whitney* and others of the Southwesterly Part of *Groton*, lie upon the Table.

[Journal of the House of Representatives (page 81), January 3, 1752.]

The Memorial of *John Whitney* and others, as entred *October* 9th 1751, Inhabitants of the Southwesterly Part of *Groton* and the Eastwardly Part of *Lunenberg*, setting forth that in *November* 1749, they preferred a Petition to this Court, praying to be set off from the Towns to which they belong, and made into a distant [distinct?] and seperate Town and Parish, for the Reasons therein mentioned ; praying that the aforesaid Memorial and Petition, with the Report of the said Committee thereon, and all the Papers thereto belonging, may be revived, and again taken into consideration.

Read again, and the Question was put, *Whether the Prayer of the Petition should be so far granted, as that the petition and Papers accompanying it should be revived ?* It pass'd in the Negative.

And *Voted*, That the Memorial be dismiss'd.

[Journal of the House of Representatives (page 92), January 9, 1752.]

The discussion in regard to the division of the town resulted in setting off the district of Shirley, on January 5, 1753, three months before the district of Pepperell was formed. In the Act of Incorporation the name was left blank, — as it was previously in the case of Harvard, and soon afterward in that of Pepperell, — and "Shirley" was filled in at the time of its engrossment. It was so named after William Shirley, the Governor of the Province at that period. It never was incorporated specifically as a town, but became one by a general Act of the Legislature, passed on March 23, 1786. It was represented, while a district, in the session of the General Court which met at Watertown on July 19, 1775, as well as in the First Provincial Congress of Massachusetts, and thus tacitly acquired the powers and privileges of a town, which were afterward confirmed by the Act just mentioned.

The enactment for establishing the district of Shirley is as follows : —

Anno Regni Regis Georgii Secundi Vicesimo Sexto.

An Act for dividing the Town of Groton and making a District by the Name of

Whereas the Inhabitants of the Southwestwardly part of the Town of Groton by Reason of the Difficulties they labour under being remote from the place of the publick worship of God have addressed this Court to be Sett off a Separate District whereunto the Inhabitants of Said Town have Manifested their Consent

Be it therefore enacted by the Lieutenant Governour Council and House of Representatives that the Southwestwardly part of the Town of Groton Comprehended within the following boundaries viz begining at the the [*sic*] mouth of Squanacook River where it runs into Lancaster [Nashua] River from thence up Said Lancaster River till it Comes to Land belonging to the Township of Stow thence Westwardly bounding Southwardly to said Stow Land till it comes to the Southwest Corner of the Township of Groton thence Northwardly bounding westwardly to Luningburgh and Townsend to Squanacook River afores[d] thence down said River and Joyning thereto to the mouth thereof being the first bound ——— Be and hereby is Sett off from the said Town of Groton and Erected into a Separate and Distinct District by the name of   and that the Inhabitants thereof be and hereby are Vested with all the powers priviledges and Immunities which the Inhabitants of any

Town within this Province do or by law ought to Enjoy Excepting only the Priviledge of choosing a Representative to represent them in the Great & General Court, in choosing of whom the Inhabitants of Said District Shall Joyn with the Inhabitants of the Town of Groton, as heretofore has been Usual, & also in paying said Representative

Provided nevertheless the Said District Shall pay their proportionable part of all such Town County Parish and Province Charges as are already Assessed upon the Town of Groton in like manner as though this Act had never been made.

And Be it further Enacted that M'ʳ Jn⁰. Whitney be and hereby is impowred to Issue his Warrant directed to Some principal Inhabitant in sᵈ District requireing Him to Notifie & warn the Inhabitants of sᵈ District qualified by law to vote in Town affairs to meet at Such Time & place as shall be therein Set forth to Choose all such officers as Shall be Necessary to manage the affairs of sᵈ District

In the House of Rep^ives June 4, 1752
Read three several times and pass'd to be Engross'd
Sent up for concurrence   T. HUBBARD Spk^r.
In Council Novr. 28, 1752 Read a first Time   29 a second Time and pass'd a Concurrence
                                  THO^S CLARKE Dp^ty Sec'ry.

[Massachusetts Archives, cxvi. 293, 294.]

This Act did not take effect until January 5, 1753, when it was signed by the Governor.

By an Act of the General Court, passed February 25, 1793, a large parcel of territory was taken from Groton and annexed to Dunstable. This change produced a very irregular boundary between the two towns, and made, according to Butler's History of Groton (page 66), more than eighty angles in the line, causing much inconvenience. The following copy from the " Laws of the Commonwealth of Massachusetts " gives the names of the families thus transferred : —

An Act to set off *Caleb Woods*, and others, from *Groton*, and to annex them to *Dunstable*.

*B*E *it enacted by the Senate and House of Representatives, in Genera] Court assembled, and by the authority of the same,* That *Caleb Woods, Silas Blood, Amaziah Swallow, Nathaniel Cummings, Eben-*

ezer *Procter*, *Silas Blood*, jun. *Silas Marshall*, *Levi Parker*, *Amos Woods*, *Isaac Lawrence*, *Peter Blood*, *Caleb Blood*, jun. *Henry Blood*, *Caleb Woods*, jun. and *Silas Marshall*, jun. together with their families and estates, and also the estates of Doctor *Jonas Marshall*, the heirs of Captain *Solomon Woods*, deceased, and *Joseph Parkhurst*, which they now own in said *Groton*, be, and they are hereby set off from the town of *Groton*, in the county of *Middlesex*, and annexed to *Dunstable*, in said county, and shall hereafter be considered a part of the same, there to do duty and receive privileges, as the other inhabitants of said *Dunstable*. *Provided nevertheless*, That the persons above-mentioned shall pay all taxes that have been legally assessed on them by said *Groton*, in the same manner as if this Act had never been passed.

[This Act passed *February* 25, 1793.]

The zigzag line caused by this Act was somewhat modified by the two following ones, passed at different times a few years later. I think that the very irregular boundary between the two towns, with its eighty-six angles, as mentioned by Mr. Butler, was produced by the subsequent annexations to Dunstable.

An Act to set of *Nathaniel Lawrence* with his Estate, from the Town of *Groton*, and annex them to the Town of *Dunstable*.

*B*E *it enacted by the Senate and House of Representatives, in General Court assembled, and by the authority of the same*, That *Nathaniel Lawrence* of *Groton*, in the county of *Middlesex*, together with his estate, which he now owns in that town, be, and hereby is set off from said town of *Groton*, and annexed to the town of *Dunstable*, in the same county; and shall hereafter be considered as part of the same; there to do duty and receive privileges as other inhabitants of said town of *Dunstable* : *Provided nevertheless*, That the said *Nathaniel Lawrence* shall be holden to pay all taxes that have been legally assessed on him by said town of *Groton*, in the same manner as if this Act had not been passed.

[This Act passed *January* 26, 1796.]

An act to set off Willard Robbins with his estate from the town of *Groton*, in the county of *Middlesex*, and to annex the same to the town of *Dunstable*, in the same county.

Sec. 1. *BE it enacted by the Senate and House of Representatives, in General Court assembled, and by the authority of the same,* That Willard Robbins, of *Groton*, in the county of Middlesex, with his estate, be, and hereby is set off from said town of *Groton*, and annexed to the town of *Dunstable*, in said county, there to do duty and receive privileges in the same manner as other inhabitants of the said town of *Dunstable*.

Sec. 2. *And be it further enacted,* That the said Willard Robbins shall be holden to pay and discharge all legal assessments and taxes, that have been assessed upon him by said town of *Groton* prior to the passing this act.

[This act passed *June* 18, 1803.]

The boundary between the two towns now remained unchanged until February 15, 1820, when another Act was passed by the Legislature making a further surrender of territory. It took a considerable parcel of land and gave it to Dunstable, thereby straightening and simplifying the jurisdictional line, which at this time formed but five angles. By these several annexations from Groton, the township of Dunstable has acquired more than one half of its present territory.

In the autumn of 1794 a plan of Groton, Pepperell, and Shirley was made by Dr. Oliver Prescott, Jr., which gives a few interesting facts. The following notes are taken from the copy now in the office of the Secretary of State, of which there is a duplicate in the possession of the town. It will be seen that Dr. Prescott refers to the land set off by the Act of February 25, 1793 : —

This Plan contains the Bounds of three Towns, viz. Groton, Pepperrell & Shirley, — all which, together with whatsoever is delineated on said Plan, was taken by an actual Survey, agreeably to a resolve of the General Court, passed June 26, 1794, & under the Inspection of the Selectmen & Committee's from the respective towns, appointed for that purpose in the month of Sept! 1794.

By OLIVER PRESCOTT, Ju! Surveyor.

The reputed distance of Groton from Cambridge [the shire-town] is Thirty two Miles, & from Boston Thirty five miles; The River Nashua is from 8 to 10 rods in width. The River Squannacoock 4 or 5 rods in width. In Groton are twenty natural Ponds, six of which are delineated on the Plan, by actual Survey. Several of the other Ponds are in size, nearly equal to those on the plan, & may in the whole contain about two Thousand Acres. There are no Mines in said Town, except one of Iron Ore, nearly exhausted. Every other Matter directed to be delineated, described or specifyed, may be found on the Plan.

Sam^{ll} Lawrence
Zach^h Fitch } Committee.
Oliver Prescott Ju^r.

The reputed distance of Pepperrell from Cambridge is thirty seven miles; from Boston forty Miles.

The River Nissitisset is about four Rods in width.

The reputed distance of Shirley from Cambridge is thirty five Miles; & from Boston thirty Eight Miles.

Catacoonamug & Mulpus Brook's are from one to two Rods in width. The Plan contains every thing relative to the two last mentioned Towns necessary to be described.

Oliver Prescott, Ju^r.

What is enclosed in this Blue line, contains about the quantity of Land set off from Groton to Dunstable, by Act of the General Court, passed February 25, 1793. As by said Act, the petitioners and their Farms were set off, without specifying particular bounds, Accuracy cannot be obtained, with respect to this Line, without very great expence and Trouble.

At the time Prescott's plan was made, a narrow strip of territory of unequal width, lying between Groton and Tyngsborough, was the subject of some controversy. The parcel of land contained not more than fifteen or twenty acres, and was claimed by both towns. On the plan it is enclosed by itself, and marked "Disputed Line." The question remained open during some years; and in the warrant for the town-meeting in May, 1801, the following article was inserted, which seems to have covered the matter in dispute: —

To choose a Committee, and give them ample power to settle and agree with the Towns of Tingsborough and Dunstable upon such regular & lasting meets and bounds as may prevent future misunderstanding respecting jurisdiction, and not interfere with, or weaken any proprietary or individual claim upon the soil, or any part thereof: or act on this article as the Town may think proper.

At the May meeting this article was considered, and a committee appointed, consisting of Oliver Prescott, Jr., Esq., Honorable Timothy Bigelow, and James Brazer, Esq. They appear to have acted with a similar committee on the part of the town of Tyngsborough, and made a joint report, bearing date October 21, 1801, which was accepted by the town of Groton on March 2, 1802.

The following extract is taken from it : —

Accordingly on the twenty-ninth day of September last, pursuant to due notice and previous agreement we did run, perambulate and renew said dividing line between said towns of Groton and Tingsborough and agreed the regular and lasting meets and bounds on said line hereafter described, viz., beginning at a pillar of Stones, the antient corner of Groton, Dunstable and Westford thence the line runs northerly about four hundred and fifty rods to a stake and stones on the easterly side of a place called dead hole, thence about one hundred and four rods to the mouth of Cow pond brook where it now empties into Massabog pond at a stake and stones, thence to the nearest corner of Dunstable and Tingsborough, the above line is the whole extent where said Towns adjoin each other.

OLIVER PRESCOTT Ju.
TIMOTHY BIGELOW
JAMES BRAZER
} Committee of Groton.

JON^A BANCROFT
JOSIAH DANFORTH
JOHN WOODWARD
} Committee of Tingsborough.

[Town Records, v. 516.]

It seems probable that a very small parcel of territory belonging to the original Groton Plantation was in this way acquired by Tyngsborough ; but how much, it is not easy to say. Danforth's survey was not sufficiently exact to make its courses and directions agree with the present boundaries of the neighboring towns.

By an Act passed February 6, 1798, a considerable portion of territory lying on the easterly side of the Nashua River, in the southwest corner of Groton, was annexed to Shirley. This tract continued to form a part of Shirley until the incorporation of Ayer, on February 14, 1871, when its political condition was again changed, and its government transferred to the new town. The Act authorizing the annexation is as follows, — and I give it entire in order to show the loose way of describing boundary lines during the latter part of the last century : —

An Act to set off certain Lands from the town of *Groton*, and annex the same to the town of *Shirley*.

SECT. 1. *BE it enacted by the Senate and House of Representatives, in General Court assembled, and by the authority of the same,* That a tract of Land at the south western extremity of the town of *Groton,* bounded by a line beginning at a large white oak stump, on the southeast side of *Nashua River,* being the northwest corner of the town of *Harvard;* thence running southeasterly on *Harvard* line, as the town bounds direct, till it comes to the stump of a pine tree lately fallen down, an antient bound mark in said town line ; thence northerly to a heap of stones by the road leading to *Harvard* at SIMON DABY's southerly corner, thence northeasterly on said SIMON DABY's line to a pine tree marked, thence northerly to a heap of stones on a ledge of rocks ; thence northerly on said SIMON DABY's line to a heap of stones on a large rock ; thence northwesterly still on said SIMON DABY's line to a stake and stones in the roots of a pine tree, fallen down, in a valley, said SIMON DABY's northeast corner and SAMUEL CHASE's southerly corner, thence northerly on said SAMUEL CHASE's line, to the road leading to ABIL MORSE's mill, at a heap of stones on the north easterly side of said road, thence northeasterly on said SAMUEL CHASE's line by said road to a heap of stones, thence northeasterly on said CHASE's line, to a stake and stones at the end of a ditch at a brook ; thence down said brook to *Nashua River,* thence up said river, to the bounds first mentioned, together with the inhabitants thereof, be, and they are hereby set off from the town of *Groton* and annexed to the town of *Shirley*, there to do duty and receive privileges in the same manner as other lands and inhabitants of the said town of *Shirley*.

SECT. 2. *Provided nevertheless, and be it further enacted,* That the said tract of land and the inhabitants thereof shall be liable to be taxed by the town of *Groton*, their full proportion in a tax to the amount of the debts now due from said town of *Groton*, in the same manner as if this act had not been passed: *Provided* such tax be made and assessed within one year from the time of passing this act; and shall also be liable to pay their proportion of all state taxes that may be assessed on the town of *Groton* until a new valuation be taken.

[This Act passed *February* 6, 1798.]

All the changes of territorial jurisdiction thus far noted have been in one direction, — from Groton to the surrounding towns; but now the tide turns, and for a wonder she receives, by legislative enactment, on February 3, 1803, a small parcel of land just large enough for a potato-patch. The annexation came from Pepperell, and the amount received was four acres and twenty rods in extent. The following is a copy: —

An act to set off a certain parcel of land from the town of *Pepperell*, in the county of *Middlesex*, and to annex the same to the town of *Groton*, in the same county.

*B*E *it enacted by the Senate and House of Representatives, in General Court assembled, and by the authority of the same,* That a certain tract of land, bounded, beginning at the end of a wall by the road leading by Zachariah Fitch's, in said *Groton;* thence running easterly, by land of Jonas Fitch, to the *Nashua River*, (so called;) thence up said river to said road, near the bridge over the same river; thence, bounding by the same road, to the bounds first mentioned, containing four acres and twenty rods, be, and hereby is set off from said town of *Pepperell* and annexed to said town of *Groton* forever.

[This act passed Feb. 3, 1803.]

The Worcester and Nashua Railroad was first opened for regular business through the township of Groton on December 18, 1848. It ran at that time a distance of eight miles through its territory, keeping on the east side of the Nashua River, which for a considerable part of the way was the dividing line between Groton and Pepperell. The railroad station for the people of Pepperell was on the Groton side of the river, and in the course of a few years a village sprang up in the neighborhood. All the interests and sympathies of this little settlement were with Pepperell; and under these circumstances the Legislature, on May 18, 1857, passed an Act of annexation, by which it became in reality what it was in sentiment, — a part and parcel of that town. The first section of the Act is as follows: —

An act to set off a part of the Town of Groton, and annex the same to the Town of Pepperell.

Be it enacted, &c., as follows:

SECTION 1. All that part of the town of Groton, in the county of Middlesex, with the inhabitants thereon, lying north of the following described line, is hereby set off from the town of Groton, and annexed to the town of Pepperell, to wit: Beginning at the boundary between said town of Groton and the town of Dunstable, at a stone monument in the wall on land of Elbridge Chapman and land of Joseph Sanderson, and running south, eighty-six degrees west, about six hundred and sixty rods, to a stone monument at the corner of land called the "Job Shattuck Farm," and land of James Hobart, near the Nashua River and Worcester and Nashua Railroad; thence in same line to the centre of Nashua River and the boundary of said town of Pepperell: *provided, however*, that for the purpose of electing a representative to the general court, the said territory shall continue to be a part of the town of Groton, until a new apportionment for representatives is made; and the inhabitants resident therein shall be entitled to vote in the choice of such representatives, and shall be eligible to the office of representative in the town of Groton, in the same manner as if this act had not been passed.

The latest legislation connected with the dismemberment of the original grant — and perhaps the last for many years to come — is the Act of February 14, 1871, by which the town of Ayer was incorporated. This enactment took from Groton a large section of territory lying near its southern borders, and from Shirley all that part of the town on the easterly side of the Nashua River which was annexed to it from Groton on February 6, 1798.

Thus has the old Groton Plantation, during a period of more than two centuries, been hewed and hacked down to less than one half of its original dimensions. Formerly it contained 40,960 acres, while now the amount of taxable land within the town is 19,850 acres. It has furnished, substantially, the entire territory of Pepperell, Shirley, and Ayer, more than one half of Dunstable, and has contributed more or less to form five other towns, — namely, Harvard, Littleton, and Westford, in Massachusetts; besides Nashua and Hollis, in New Hampshire. The present shape of the town is very irregular, and all the original boundary lines have been changed except where they touch Townsend and Tyngsborough. An examination of the map opposite to the titlepage of this book will show these changes more clearly than any verbal or written description.

INDEX.

ADAMS, WILLIAM, 55, 59.
Addington, Isaac, 24, 26.
Allen, William, (Allin) 58; 73, 75.
Ames, Jacob, 75.
Ames, John, 12, 30.
Andover, Mass., 10.
Apostle Eliot, 19.
Atherton, Amos, 84.
Ayer, Mass., 10, 33; incorporation of, 95, 98.

BALDWIN, JEREMIAH, 55.
Baldwin, Samuel, 55.
Bancroft, Jonathan, 94.
Barker, John, 24.
Bartlit, Caleb, 85.
Barton, Henry, 55.
Bateman, John, 24.
Beaver Brook, mention of, in Dunstable land grant, 17; mention of, in Harvard Incorporation Act, 50.
Becket, Mass., 41.
Belcher, Jonathan, Governor of Massachusetts, 35, 48, 49, 51, 53, 56, 57, 58, 60.
Belcher's Grant, 41.
Bennett, Moses, Jr., 85.
Berry, Thomas, 57.
Bigelow, Jonathan, 84.
Bigelow, Joshua, 42.
Bigelow, Hon. Timothy, 94.
Billerica, Mass., 10, 14, 15.

Blanchard, Capt., 34.
Blanchard, Joseph, 55, 69.
Blanchard, William, 59.
Blanford, Mass., 40.
Blood, Caleb, Jr., 91.
Blood, David, 75.
Blood, Henry, 91.
Blood, James, Jr., 74.
Blood, John, 62.
Blood, John, Jr., 75.
Blood, Joseph, 62.
Blood, Josiah, 55, 59.
Blood, Nathaniel, 55.
Blood, Peter, 91.
Blood, Silas, 90.
Blood, Silas, Jr., 91.
Blood, Solomon, 74.
Blood, William, 58, 73.
Bond, Joseph, 84.
Boston Farms, 14, 15.
Boundaries, of Old Groton, 9; importance of, to communities and individuals, 9; principle of, as embodied in the Mosaic Code of laws, 9; principle of, personified and deified by ancient Romans, 9.
Boxborough, Mass., 16.
Brattle, Major William, 46.
Brazer, James, 94.
Brewer, Mr., 67.
Brookline, N. H., 33, 36.
Brown Hill, 25, 29.
Brown, Hannah, 84.

Brown, Capt. Hopestill, 28, 29.
Brown, Joseph, 84.
Browne, Samuel, 55.
Browne, W., 55.
Buck Meadow, 14, 15.
Buckminster, Col. Joseph, 42.
Bulkeley, Col. John, 39.
Burk, John, 48.
Burk, John, Jr., 48.
Burnap, Joseph, 28, 29.
Burrell, Ebenezer, 47.
Burrell, John, 24.
Burt, Phinehas, 85.
Butler, Caleb, 13, 33; his History of Groton quoted, 64; cited, 90, 91.
Buttrick, John, 24.

CHAMBERLIN, JOHN, 62, 74.
Chambrlin, Phineahas, 74.
Chandler, Col. John, 34, 87.
Chandler, Samuel, 46.
Chandler's Grant, 41.
Chapman, Elbridge, 97.
Charlestown School Farm, mention of, in Dunstable land grant, 17.
Chase, Samuel, 95.
Chelmsford, Mass., 10, 14, 15, 17; joint petition of, to General Court regarding Nashobah territory, 23, 25.
Clap, Col. Thomas, 42.
Clarke, Thomas, 81, 90.
Colburn, Isaac, 67.
Colburn, James, 77, 78.
Colburn, Robert, 55.
Colburn, William, 55.
Collans, John, 69.
Concord, Mass., 22; joint petition of, to General Court regarding Nashobah territory, 23, 25.
Cowell, Edward, 14, 15.
Coyachus, 34.
Coyecus Brook, 83.
Cumings, James, 55.
Cumings, Jerahmal, 55.
Cumings, John, 62, 74.
Cumings, Samuel, 59, (Comings) 69, 71.
Cumings, William, 62.
Cummings, Capt., 67, (Cummins) 68.
Cummings, Nathaniel, 90.
Cushing, Thomas, 74, 76.

DABEY, SIMON, 95.
Danforth, Jonathan, 30; first appointment by General Court as surveyor of Groton, 10; his resignation and second appointment to same duties, 10, 11; poetical tribute to his character, 11.
Danforth, Josiah, 94.
Danforth, Samuel, 12, 30.
Darby, John, 24.
Davis, Eleazer, 47; a survivor of Lovewell's Fight at Pequawket, 48; pension granted to, 48.
Davis, John, 48.
Dinsmoor, Thos., 55, (Dinsmore) 62.
Divoll, Manasser, 84.
Dodge, Joseph, 85.
Doublet, Sarah, *alias* Sarah Indian, 28.
Dram Cup Hill, mention of, in Dunstable land grant, 17, 35, 36.
Dudley, Joseph, 22, 23, 28, 29.
Dunstable, Mass., 10, 16, 32, 34; original grant of, 17; inaccuracies of early map of, 18; incorporation of, 18; West Parish of, 58; division of, by Provincial Line, 63; partial annexation of, to Nottingham, 63; location of meeting-house at, and excitement attendant thereon, 64-68; attempted annexation of part of Nottingham and the Joint Grass district to, 64-69; final success thereof, 70, 71; partial annexation to Pepperell, 76, 77; partial annexation of Groton land to, and establishment of boundary line with that town, 90-92.

EAMES, STEPHEN, 59, (Ames) 61.
East Pepperell, Mass., 14.
Eaton, Joseph, 55.
Ellat, Elies, 74, (Elias Ellit) 75.
Emerson, Rev. Joseph, cited, 64, 78.
Epes, Major Daniel, 34.

FARLE, SAMUEL, 59.
Farley, Benjamin, 55.
Farmer, William, 84.
Farmer & Moore's "Collections," extract from, 11.

… INDEX. 101

Farmington River, 40, 41.
Farneth, William, 85.
Farnsworth, Daniel, 47.
Farnsworth, Ephraim, 47.
Farnsworth, Jeremiah, 47.
Farnsworth, Jonathan, Jr., 47.
Farnsworth, Phenihas, 84.
Farnsworth, Reuben, 47.
Farnworth, Simeon, 84.
Farwell, Almer, 85.
Farwell, Henery, 85.
Farwell, Isaac, 55.
Farwell, John, 83.
Farwell, Josiah, 85.
Fisk, Nathan, 74.
Fisk, Samuel, 58, 74.
Fisk, Thomas, 62.
Fitch, Jonas, 96.
Fitch, Zachariah, 93, 96.
Flegg, Eleazer, 59.
Fletcher, Hezekiah, 24.
Fletcher, Joseph, 24, 69, 71.
Fletcher, Robert, 69.
Flint, Lieut. John, 19, 20, (Flynt) 25.
Flood, Samuel, 84.
Forge Pond, 13, 16, 45.
Fowle, John, Jr., 55.
Fox, Mr. Jabez, 65.
Foxcroft, Francis, 65.
Frost, Abijah, 84.
Frost, Simon, 56, 57.
Fryeburg, Me., 48.

GENERAL COURT, grants land for township of Groton, 9; its selection of surveyors for laying out Groton township, 10, 11; petitions submitted to, regarding disputed Nashobah territory, 19, 22, 23, 25, 27; confirmation of original Groton land grant by, 26, 30; final re-establishment of Nashobah as township by, 27.
Gerrish, Col. Joseph, 42, 65.
Gilson, Ebenezer, 58, 74, 75.
Gould, David, 85.
Gould, Jonathan, 85.
Gould, Samuel, 69.
Green, Eleazer, 75.
Green, James, 62, 75.
Green, John, 59, 61.

Greenleaf, John, 88.
Greenville, N. H., 34, 36.
Groton, early boundary lines of, 9-18; original grant of township, 9, 10; surveyors appointed by General Court for laying out township of, 10, 11; making of its survey and troubles incidental thereto, 10, 11; plans of its survey, 11, 12, 13; plan of early township as now existing, 13, 14; incorporation of, 18; encroachments of, on abandoned Nashobah territory, 21, 22; confirmation of original land grant of, by General Court, 26, 30; its loss from the Nashobah settlement of boundaries, 32; application for grant of Groton Gore, 32; General Court Record of grant of Gore, 35, 36; boundaries of Gore, 36; subsequent loss of Gore by decision regarding Provincial Line, 38, 39; equivalent grant of land to, with description thereof, 39-41; partial annexation of territory to Westford, 45; partial annexation of territory to Littleton, 51; petitions for and against further dismemberment of, in favor of Hollis, 53-62; attempted annexation of Joint Grass district of, to Dunstable, 65-69; final success thereof, 70; petitions for establishment of West Parish as separate precinct of, 72-76; final establishment of West Parish as separate district and town, 78-81; petitions for further division of, in favor of Shirley, 82-88; partial annexation of, to Dunstable, and establishment of boundary line with that town, 90-92; Prescott's plan of, 92-94; unsuccessful land dispute with Tyngsborough, 93, 94; further annexation of land to Shirley, 95, 96; acquisition of Pepperell land by, 96; opening of Worcester & Nashua R. R., and consequent loss of land by partial annexation to Pepperell, 97; further dismemberment of, with incorporation of Ayer, 98; comparison between the early and present territory of, 98.
Groton Old Corner, 16.

INDEX.

Hale, Mr. Robert, 34, 48.
Hall, Richard, 84.
Hall, Timothy, 84.
Harris, Francis, 85.
Harris, Stephen, 55.
Hartewell, Samuel, Jr., 24.
Hartwell, Edward, 87.
Harvard, Mass., 10; incorporation and make-up of, with first petition therefor, 46; early plan of, as now existing, 47; final petition for incorporation, 48; Act of Incorporation of, 50, 51; petition for division of, in favor of Shirley, 82-88.
Haskell, Henry, 84.
Hauthorne, William, 63.
Haverhill, Mass., 10, 16.
Hazen, Samuel, 84.
Heald, John, 24.
Hell Pond, 83, 84.
Henchman, Mr., 27.
Henry, Robert, 83, 85.
Heywood, John, 24.
Hill, John, 65, 70.
Hill, John Boynton, cited, 37.
Hinchman, Capt. Thomas, 19.
Hobart, Gershom, 74.
Hobart, James, 97.
Hobson, Capt. John, 34, 55.
Hodgman, Rev. Edwin Rutherford, his History of Westford quoted, 45.
Holdin, Caleb, 85.
Holdin, Isaac, 85.
Holdin, Philemon, 85.
Holdin, Stephen, Jr., 85.
Hollis, N. H., 10, 16, 58.
Holten, Dr. Samuel, 42.
Horse Pond, 83.
Houghton, Jacob, 47, 84.
Houghton, John, Jr., 84.
Houghton, Jonas, 35, 46, 47, (Haughton) 48; 49.
Housatonick townships, 41.
Howe, Gideon, 59.
Howe, Thomas, 24, (How) 26.
Hubbard, Thomas, 78, 81, 90.
Hubburd, Jonathan, 24.
Hunt, Enoch, 59.
Hutchins, Joseph, 84.

Ipswich, Mass., 35, 36; grant of land to, 36.

Jeffs, Henery, 62.
Jeffries, John, 52.
Jereinies Hill, mention of, in Dunstable land grant, 17.
Jewett, Nehemiah, 75.
Johnson, Joshua, 84.
Joint Grass, 65.
Jones, Maj. John, 65, 87.
Jones, Samuel, 24.

Keen, Wm., 24.
Kelcey, John, 85.
Kemp, John, 75.
Kent, Abner, 45.
Kindal, Relph, 83.

Lakin, Isaac, 62, 74.
Lakin, Jacob, 62, 74.
Lancaster, Mr. Thomas, 42.
Lancaster, Mass., 10, 22, 47; joint petition to General Court regarding Nashobah territory, 23, 25; petition for division of, in favor of Shirley, 82-88.
Larwance, Enoch, 62, (Lawarnce) 73.
Larwance, James, 62, 74.
Laughton, Thomas, 85.
Laurance, Joseph, 74.
Lawrence, Isaac, 91.
Lawrence, Jeremiah, 59, (Lawrance) 73; 75, (Jarimah Lawrance) 77.
Lawrence, Maj. William, 67.
Lawrence, Nathaniel, 91.
Lawrence, Nathaniel, Jr., 62.
Lawrence, Peleg, 20, 21, (Lawrance) 77.
Lawrence, Peter, 52.
Lawrence, Samuel, 67.
Lawrence, William, 60, 71.
Lawrence, Zachariah, Jr., 59, (Lawrance) 73, (Zachery) 75.
Lemmon, Joseph, 55.
Leominster, Mass., 16, 86.
Leveret, Rev. John, 28.
Littleton, Mass., 10, 16 (see Nashobah).
Livermore, Capt. Samuel, 87.
Longley, John, Jr., 84.
Longley, Jonas, 85.
Lovewell, Capt. John, 48.
Lovewell's Pond, 15.
Lunenberg, Mass., 86, 87, 88, (Luningburgh) 89.

INDEX.   103

MALVEN, JOHN, 55.
Malven, Jonathan, 55.
Marshall, Dr. Jonas, 91.
Marshall, Silas, 91.
Marshall, Silas, Jr., 91.
Mason, N. H., 33, 36..
Massachusetts Archives, extract from, 22, 23, 25, 49, 52, 56, 57, 59, 60, 62, 67, 69, 74, 76, 78, 81, 84, 90.
Massachusetts House of Representatives, extract from Journal of, 34, 36, 39, 41, 42, 43, 45, 46, 47, 49, 52, 65, 66, 68, 70, 71, 86, 87, 88.
Massapoag Pond, 14, 16, 18.
Meers, Capt. Robt., 27.
Merrimack River, mention of, in Dunstable land grant, 17; 37.
Merryfield, Mass., 40.
Middlefield, Mass., Memorial of Hundredth Anniversary cited, 43.
Miles, John, 24.
Milford, N. H., 34, 36.
Millstone Hill, 45.
Minot, James, 55, 67, 87.
Miriam, John, 24.
Moodey, Mr. Samuel, 48.
Morse, Abel, 95.
Mosaic Code of laws, its embodiment of the principle of fixed boundaries, 9.
Mozier, John, 75.

NASHOBAH, 14, 16; township grant to Indians, 19; subsequent abandonment of, 19; early controversies regarding territory of, 19, 21, 22, 23, 27; re-establishment of boundary lines of, 19, 29; various petitions to General Court regarding territory of, 19, 22, 23, 25, 27; township, re-establishment of, 26, 27; reservation by General Court in favor of descendants of early Indian proprietors of, 28, 29; incorporation of, 29; change of name to Littleton, 29.
Nashua, N. H., 10, 15, 18.
Nashua River, 13, 14, 16, 54, 56, 95; early names for, 63.
Nason's History of Dunstable cited, 69.
Navins, Thomas, 55.
Nicholls, John, 84.
Nickols, Col. Ebenezer, 42.

Nissitissett Hills, 14, 18.
Nonacoicus, 32, 85, (Coyachus) 34.
Nottingham, incorporation and territory of, 63; division of, by Provincial Line, and change of name of N. H. part, 63; attempted partial annexation of, to Dunstable, 64, 65, 66, 68, 69.
Noyes, Ensign Peter, begins survey of Groton, 10; his death, 10.

OAK HILLS, 16.
Osgood, John, 84.
Otis, John, 87.

PAGE, DANIEL, 83, 84, 85.
Park, James, 85.
Parker, Benjamin, 62, 74.
Parker, Josiah, 75.
Parker, Levi, 91.
Parker, Lieut. Nathaniel, 39, 61, 73.
Parker, Obadiah, 55.
Parker, Phiniahas, Jr., 74.
Parker, Samuel, 59.
Parkhurst, Ebenezer, 67, 71.
Parkhurst, Joseph, 69, 71, 91.
Parlin, John, 24.
Pattorson, James, 85.
Pawer, Peter, 55, 62.
Pawtucket Falls, Mass., 38.
Pearce, Ebenezer, 55, (Peirce) 58, (Parce) 74.
Pearce, John, 84.
Pemigewasset River, 37.
Pepperell, Mass., 10, 14; extract from dedication sermon at second meeting-house in, 64; incorporation and naming of, 78-81; early limitations of the town privileges of, 79; Prescott's plan of, 92-94; loss of small tract of territory annexed to Groton, 96; annexation of Groton land to, 97.
Pepperrell, Sir William, 78.
Pequawket, Lovewell's Fight at, 48.
Perham, Joseph, (Perriaham) 69.
Phillips, Seth, 62, 74.
Phips, Spencer, 28, (Phipes) 77; 78.
Pierce, Daniel, 87.
Power, Jerathmel, 85.
Powers, Daniel, 21.

Powers, Walter, 21.
Powers, William, 24.
Preist, Joseph, 84.
Prescott, Hon. Benj., 32, 42, 77.
Prescott, Ebenezer, 45.
Prescott, Hon. James, 13, 33.
Prescott, James, (Prescot) 39; 41, 42.
Prescott, Capt. Jonas, 21, (Prescot) 45; 47.
Prescott, Oliver, 39; joint petition for land grant, 41, 42.
Prescott, Dr. Oliver, Jr., 94; plan of Groton, Pepperell, and Shirley by, 92, 93.
Prescott, William, 39, 76; joint petition for land grant, 41, 42, 77.
Preston, William, 85.
Priest, Joseph, 84.
Procter, Ebenezer, 55, 91.
Procter, Gershom, 24.
Procter, John, 24.
Procter, Moses, 55.
Procter, Samuel, 24.
Provincial Line, 32, 33; the subject of dispute, 37, 38; definite settlement of, and consequent loss of territory to Groton, 38, 39.

QUINCY, J., Speaker of House of Representatives, 49, 51, 56, 57, 59, 65.

RANDAL, SAMUEL, 84.
Rand's Grant, 41.
Read, Jonathan, 84.
Read, Jonathan, Jr., 84.
Read, Timothy, 69, 71.
Reed, Ralph, 33, (Read) 39.
Remant, Daniel, 55.
Rice, Mr. Phineas, 87.
Richards, Charles, 84.
Richards, Col. Joseph, 87.
Ridge Road, 15.
Right, Samuel, (Wright) 73.
Robbins, Benjamin, 62, 69, 71, (Robins) 74.
Robbins, Eleazer, 47.
Robbins, Robert, 20, 21, (Robins) 24.
Robbins, Willard, 92.
Russell, John, 48, 85.
Russll, Amos, 84.

SACO RIVER, 43.
Saltonstall, Nathaniel, 55.
Sampson, Benjamin, 84.
Sampson, John, 84.
Sanderson, Joseph, 97.
Sartell, Josiah, 33, (Sawtell) 39; 62, 74.
Sartell, Nathaniel, 51, 52, 60.
Sawtell, Hezekiah, Jr., 85.
Sawtelle, Ithamar Bard, cited, 33.
Sawyer, Corp. Elias, 84.
Scott, John, 62.
Shadd, John, 75.
Shattuck, David, 62, 75.
Shattuck, James, 62, 75.
Shattuck, John, 62.
Shattuck, Jonathan, 62, 75.
Shattuck, Jonathan, Jr., 62, 75.
Shattuck, Samuel, Jr., 62, 75.
Shattuck, William, 55.
Sheple, Jona., Groton Town Clerk, 60.
Shepley, John, 12, 30.
Shirley, Mass., 10, 16; attempts at formation of precinct from Groton, Lancaster, and Harvard lands, 82–88; Act of Incorporation of, 89, 90; Prescott's plan of, 92–94; annexation of Groton land to, 95, 96.
Shirley, William, Governor of Massachusetts, 66, 72, 74, 76, 89.
Shute, Samuel, 31.
Simonds, William, 85.
Smith, Prof. Edward Payson, quoted, 44.
Souhegan River, mention of, in Dunstable land grant, 17; (Sohegan) 35, 36, 56.
Spaulding, John, 74.
Spaulding, Joseph, Jr., (Spoaldeng) 62; (Spalding) 69; 71, 73, 74.
Spaulding, Zacheus, 69.
Spoalding, William, 62, (Spalden) 75.
Squannacook River, 18, 85, 89.
Stearns, John, (Sternes) 24; 25.
Stevens, Thomas, 22.
Stone, James, 51.
Stone, Simon, 46.
Stone, Simon, Jr., 47, 48, (Stoon) 49.
Stony Brook Pond, 13, 45.
Stow Leg, 16, 82.
Stow, Mass., petition to General Court regarding the Nashobah territory, 22–25.
Stratton, Samuel, 24.

INDEX.

Sudbury, Mass., 22.
Swallow, Amaziah, 90.
Swallow, Benjamin, 58, 61, 74, 75.
Swallow, John, 62, 65, 69, 71, 74.
Swallow, Joseph, 74.

TARBELL, THOMAS, 86.
Taylor, Abraham, Jr., 55, 62.
Taylor's Grant, 40.
Taylor, Joseph, 55.
Terminus, Roman personification of the principle of fixed boundaries, 9.
Terry, Mr. Ebenezer, 48.
Tompson, Simon, 67, (Thompson) 68.
Townsend, Mass., 32, (Townshend) 34.
Townsend, Ebenezer, 45.
Tucker, Josiah, 59, 61. 74, 75.
Turner, Mr. Israel, 87.
Tyng, Jonathan, 24, 26.
Tyng, John, 66, 67, 87.
Tyng's Corner, 45.
Tyngsborough, Mass., 16, 45; acquisition of land from Nottingham, 64; land dispute with and acquisition of land from Groton, 93, 94.

VARNUM, JONAS, 75.
Vering, David, 55.

WARNER, JOSEPH, 74.
Warner, Richard, 58. 59, 62, 74.
Watertown, Mass., Session of General Court at, 89.
Watts, Samuel, 86, 87.
Westford, Mass., 10; acquisition of Groton territory, 45.
Wheeler, Lieut. Joseph, 19, 20, (Wheler) 25.
Wheeler, Peter, 55.

Wheeler, Thomas, 24, 46, 48, (Wheler) 49.
Whit, John, 83.
Whitcomb, Josiah, 24.
Whitney, John, 85, 87, 88, 90.
Whitney, Jonathan, 46, 48, 49.
Whitney, Rev. Peter, his History of Worcester County cited, 84.
Wilder, Joseph, 65, 87.
Willard, Abijah, 84.
Willard, Benjamin, 84.
Willard, Daniel, 84.
Willard, Henry, 84.
Willard, J., 49, 50, 51, 57, 74, 76, 78.
Willard, Major Simon, 12, 32, 39, 63.
Willard, William, 84.
Williams, Col. Elijah, 42.
Williams, Isaac, 58, 74, 75.
Williams, Jacob, 85.
Williams, John, 85.
Williams, John, Jr, 85.
Williams, William, 85.
Wilson, Joseph, 85.
Wilson, Samuel, 50.
Wilton, N. H., 34, 36.
Wily, Timothy, 28, 29.
Winnepesaukee River, 37.
Winthrop, Deane, 10, 30, 34.
Wistequassuck, 63.
Wood, Addison, 16.
Woods, Amos, 91.
Woods, Caleb, 90.
Woods, Caleb, Jr., 91.
Woods, Isaac, 62, 74.
Woods, John, 62, 74.
Woods, Jonathan, 62, 75.
Woods, Moses, 75.
Woods, Solomon, 91.
Woodward, John, 94.
Woolcut's Grant, 40.
Woolerick, Philip, 55, (Wolrich) 59.
Wright, Samuel, 62, (Right) 73.
Wright, Thomas, 84.

www.ingramcontent.com/pod-product-compliance
Lightning Source LLC
Chambersburg PA
CBHW020152170426
43199CB00010B/1001